Synthesis

How Hegelian Logic has Moved the Protestant

Churches Towards a Christless Faith

By Maria Brusco Osso

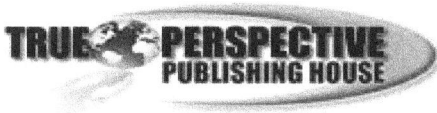

TRUE PERSPECTIVE
PUBLISHING HOUSE

Synthesis: How Hegelian Logic has Moved the Protestant Churches Towards a Christless Faith

Printed in the United States of America

ISBN 978-0-9859892-5-5

Cover Design by Marco Diaz

DEDICATION

To the Lord, my God who inspired me through the verse in Acts 19:2,

"And he said to them, 'Did you receive the Holy Spirit when you believed?' And they said, 'No we have not even heard that there is a Holy Spirit."

TABLE OF CONTENTS

PREFACE

The purpose of this book is not so much to explain or reiterate Biblical concepts but to illuminate your mind to the devastating efforts in play to undermine the Church, the Body of Christ. The current driving force that girds these dangers is found in Hegelian Dialect or logic.

Hegelian logic is being used literally to replace conventional logic. One may ask, "How has this been done unbeknownst to me?" The book outlines this phenomena and how Hegelian logic has driven the church to its present situation with the goal of replacing Christianity with a Christless faith.

One may ask, "Well what is the current situation with the Church?" The answer is that it is under attack. One may retort by stating that throughout history, the Christian church has been under attack. What is new today? My reply is, "The attack today has a different strategy." In the past, the Church had been under siege in the form of force in order to overtake or simply to wipe out the Church.

The goal of this book is to identify the attack within our churches and describe how the attack is a process used to move the church towards a Christless religion. Today the attack is in the form of changing the perception of reality within the members of the Church from a heart that is rooted in Christ to one that is Christless or secular.

Dietrich Bonhoeffer, a Lutheran theologian noted that the process of rendering the church Christless is to sever the ties between God and man and between man and reality. He understood this very well as he lived and eventually was executed for his positions during WWII. He witnessed Nazism's attempts to capture the churches in Germany and throughout the world in order to indoctrinate them with Nazi ideology.

The new way of perceiving reality underpins the current dynamics of the postmodern era in which we live in. Hegelian logic is the driving force against Christianity to propel it to a post-Christian age. Postmodernists decry and even eliminate claims to truths. Postmodern views assume that no person can know complete and perfect truth. Even attempts to discredit history have been made. This is in direct contrast to Scriptures which advocates absolute truth (John 8:31, 17:17). Changing one's perception of reality is accomplished by changing one's reasoning process or logic.

Hegelian logic which lends structure to Postmodernism is firmly established in academia and is gaining momentum in all aspects of society including the church and the way of worshipping. The book will look at events beginning in the 1960's to the present, through the lens of Hegelian logic or dialect. For it is through these lenses that one can discern how changes are mobilized to extract the cross of Jesus Christ from the churches and our lives.

Recent surveys and polls show that Americans are increasingly identifying themselves as atheists or agnostic. Atheism has become the new norm. "In other words, atheism now appears to be far more of a legitimate cultural option than the case even in the last years of the twentieth century."[1] Unfortunately, how do we as Christians respond to this growing number? Tolerance is not the answer.

The notion of tolerance whose mantra is "it does not matter what you believe, as long as you believe it sincerely', is shaping how secular society views reality."[2] In the zeal to balance tolerance and hurting any one's feelings, the belief is that the admonishment of a person's personal beliefs especially religious beliefs may leave one feeling castigated.

Nevertheless, what takes place when confronting spiritual issues is not tolerance but affirmation. A well-known contemporary Baptist theologian Albert Mohler, Jr. stated, "That our culture is really pursuing affirmation and not toleration can be seen in the outrage that is voiced any time Christians tell the media that Jesus is the only way to the Father (John 14:6)."[3]

Since the nineteenth century the orthodoxy found in the Christian churches have given way to tolerance. Over the years, through various philosophical and cultural changes, Christianity was reinterpreted for the sake of

---

[1] Albert Mohler, Jr., *Atheism Remix* (Illinois: Crossway Books, 2008), 12.
[2] Robert Rothwell, "A Brace New World," *Tabletalk* 32 (2008): 11.
[3] Albert Mohler, Jr., *Atheism Remix,* 16.

securing its survival. "The result was a series of 'Christianity's'…that bore more resemblance to the cultural norm of the day than to the historic faith of the apostles."[4] Additionally faith has taken shape in a type of "spirituality" that comes in a form of non - theistic or barely theistic beliefs that are replacing organized religion.[5]

The reinterpretation of Christianity and the "spirituality" that is occurring today is not new as it existed in Biblical times and in the early church. Romans 1:18-23, 32 states,

> *For the wrath of God is revealed from heaven against all ungodliness and unrighteousness of men, who by their unrighteousness suppress the truth. For what can be known about God is plain to them because God has shown it to them. For his invisible attributes, namely, his eternal power and divine nature, have been clearly perceived ever since the creation of the world, in the things that have been made. For although they know God, they did not know him as God or give thanks to Him, but they became futile in their thinking and their foolish hearts were darkened. Claiming to be wise, they became fools and exchanged the glory of the immortal God for images resembling mortal man and birds and animal and creeping things. Though they know God's decree that those who practice such*

---

[4] Andrew Hoffecker, "Breaking Boundaries" *Tabletalk* 32 (2008):16.
[5] Albert Mohler, Jr., *Atheism Remix,* 16.

things deserve to die, they not only do them but gave approval to those who practice them.

In the book of Revelation, Jesus rebuked the churches that succumbed to pitfalls and compromise. The dangers that those churches experienced in their spiritual strength are present today and threaten us. "Those include such things as a lack of love, a lack of truth, a compromising spirit with the world, a lukewarm devotion, and a double-minded conviction, to name a few."[6] As a counter, the Lord has also given us instructions in the book of Acts to maintain the church as the body of Christ.

Early church fathers, Tertullian and Irenaeus both documented that the early Christian church taught along the Pauline line of a unified message. "Irenaeus wrote in 185 A.D. that 'although the church was scattered throughout the world, it occupies but one house, and believes as if it had but one mind, and preaches as if it had but one mouth. And although there are many dialects in the world, the meaning of the tradition is one and the same.'"[7] If the early church was able to function with one voice, why can it not do so today? If the early Christians were unified in one message of Truth, why can't we do the same? The answer is that we can. We just need to be diligent, attentive, and equip ourselves in order to deter the malicious wave of "change" that is engulfing the Churches.

---

[6] R. C. Sproul, "Perils Facing the Evangelical Church" Tabletalk 33 (2009): 7.
[7] Andrew Hoffecker, "Breaking Boundaries" *Tabletalk* 32 (2008): 15.

Our task at hand is to prevent ourselves from diverging from God's Word; focusing always on glorifying Him.

Today we have the Holy Spirit that guides the Church to maintain itself as the Body of Christ. It provides the unity in churches. The early church developed the value of unity even before the Holy Spirit came to the early Christians. Unity was exemplified as "All those with one accord were devoting themselves to prayer together with the women and Mary the mother of Jesus and his brothers" (Acts 1:14). The early church followers knew that not only did they have to stay together and act as one; not only in their being, but also in their actions. By their lifestyle, others took note and were amazed. They started to observe, listen and ask questions.

Christianity today has many challenges and it is each Christians' duty to respond to opposition. The weapon against such opposition is the Word of God, the sword. If one cannot tell someone that what they are doing is against God's law, how can one preach the good news of salvation? The postmodern sentiment has transcended into the churches to reflect a Christless faith. A Christless faith emphasizes the carnality of Jesus over His deity and denies His role as the Messiah (the Christ). No messiah, no indwelling Holy Spirit that tells us the will of the Lord, our God. Replacing the Messiah is man. The break between man and God and between man and reality is accomplished. Evil will gladly step in.

CHAPTER ONE

❦ ❦ ❦

GROUNDWORK

"If evil appears in the form of light, benefit, loyalty, and renewal, if it conforms with historical necessity and social justice, then this, if it is understood straightforwardly is a clear proof of its abysmal wickedness." [8] Dietrich Bonhoeffer

During WWII Dietrich Bonhoeffer, German theologian, pastor and martyr penned the aforementioned words during the Nazi revolution in Germany. Words such as benefit, renewal and social justice continue to echo today. At the Trinity Lutheran Church in Berlin, Germany Bonhoeffer strove to awake the congregation to what was happening within the church as well as outside the church. As he tried to wave the smelling salts under the snoozing churches' nose he adamantly declared, "For the times, which are the times of collapse to the human understanding may well be for her a great time of building…Church, remain a church…

---

[8]Dietrich Bonhoeffer, *Ethics* (New York: Touchstone Books, 1995).

Confess! Confess! Confess!" (Proclaim the Gospel). The time Bonhoeffer is proclaiming is also at hand.

At the height of Nazism, Hitler had a stranglehold on the church, both spiritually and politically. Hitler tried to deceive the nation of Germany and had a plan to do it. He issued orders, laws, changed the German Constitution, and through propaganda considered all tangible ways to bring down the Christian church. These efforts included the murder of hundreds if not thousands of pastors of which Dietrich Bonhoeffer was one.

Hitler's downfall was his impatience for world domination and through force he literally pounded the church into submission and acceptance of his "religion." He did not succeed because there were people filled with the Holy Spirit, who were willing to endure pain, suffering, and risk death for the sake of the Church.

Thus, Satan's plan to dominate the world through Hitler came to an abrupt halt in April of 1945. Satan was forced to go back to the drawing board. His plan had failed. Astute Christians today are aware of Satan and his deceptive ways but they are not aware of his deep and most deceptive plan yet. The plan appears to be not so dissimilar to his first plan to slither into Christian theology with words such as social justice, freedom, liberty, happiness, and equality. Reread what Bonhoeffer said in the beginning of this chapter. Seventy odd years ago he read the writing on the wall and understood it!

Times have not changed since then. The same writing is still on the wall. But will we be able to understand it today? In Germany, Hitler introduced the same concepts of liberation, freedom, equality, and social justice at a time when the German nation was striving in economic disaster. The population was willing to sell their souls to Hitler so they could have job security and food on their tables. Will we do the same today? We already have job and financial insecurity, poverty, and unemployment. Will we follow suit like the Germans?

In the early 1990's, the late Dr. D. James Kennedy, senior pastor at Coral Ridge Presbyterian Church in Fort Lauderdale, Florida, alerted his church. He warned congregants to be on the lookout for "infiltrators" in the church whose aim is to change its direction away from God's chosen path. As a result of these "infiltrators" and changes in theology brought about in the academic colleges and seminaries, mainline churches such as the Presbyterians, Episcopalians, Lutherans, and Methodists, have caved in, forsaking Scriptural truths in the name of liberation, freedom, equality, and social justice. As a result, we now have tolerance for gay and lesbian pastors, feminist agendas, gay and lesbian marriage, hell reduced to a level that it really does not exist at all, no sin, and the incomplete concept "God loves us all." The plan the "infiltrators are using could be likened to Brian McLaren's, founder of the "Emerging Church Movement's," fifteen to twenty year plan to change the churches from within (the plan will be discussed in later chapters).

Thomas Hobbes, an English philosopher, stated in his book, *Leviathan,* "Powers invisible and supernatural…can never be so abolished out of human nature, but that new Religions may again be made to spring out of them."[9] Just like Hobbes, Satan is aware of the innate human desire for the supernatural. According to Satan it just needs to be controlled and directed. The question is how can it be done? The attempt is to change the way man views realty.

GRACE

"We Lutherans have gathered like eagles around the carcass of cheap grace and there we have drunk poison which has killed the life of following Christ."[10]

Cheap grace[11] according to Bonhoeffer, has brought the collapse of organized churches. It has done this by selling whole-sale true grace to our humanitarian sentiments such as tolerance, justice, equality, and freedom. He writes, "We pour forth unending streams of grace. But the call to follow Jesus in the narrow way was hardly heard. Where were those truths which impelled the early church to institute the catechumenate" [the beginners in Christianity] "which enabled a strict watch to be kept over the frontier between the Church and the world, and

---

[9] Thomas Hobbs (1588 – 1679) an English philosopher who is well known for his work in political philosophy. His book, Leviathan (1651) provided the foundation for Western political philosophy. Leviathan is a free download at www.gutenberg.org/etext/3207.
[10] Dietrich Bonhoeffer, *The Cost of Discipleship* (New York: Macmillan, 1966), 44.
[11] Ibid.

afforded adequate protection for costly grace?"[12] Grace is costly because it is through Jesus' sacrifice that God offers it to us. Grace is not freely offered to whomever; it requires faith as opposed to self-reliance. If one is to receive this costly grace, one has to believe not in himself as in self-reliance, but in another and the other is Jesus Christ. Rom. 3:23-25 states, *"for all have sinned and fall short of the glory of God and are justified by his grace as a gift through the redemption that is in Christ Jesus whom God put forth as a propitiation by his blood, to be received by faith."* The grace of God is demonstrated by his divine forbearance as he passes over former sins.

The consequence of cheap grace is the disillusionment that it offers. Instead of allowing us to hear the call of the Holy Spirit to follow Jesus, we are offered a "journey of spirituality." Instead of the call to discipleship, we are presented with a pedestrian way of our choosing. We do not have to expend any energy. Hey, the work was already done by Jesus! All we need to do is set Him up as the model for living our life on earth.

JUSTIFICATION

Bonhoeffer cries out, **"Satan has gained into the Church and is trying to tear it away from the cross of its Lord [!]"[13]** He does this through the reinterpretation of the doctrine of justification and other foundational doctrines.

---

[12] Ibid.
[13] Bonhoeffer, *The Cost of Discipleship*, 77

Exactly what is justification? It is a process whereby after we are called by God to trust in Jesus for salvation, God gives us a spiritual awakening.

We respond to this spiritual awakening by faith in Jesus and repentance for our sins. God graciously acts in response to our faith as promised, by declaring our sins forgiven. The core emphasis of the doctrine of justification is how believers, despite their sin, can stand before God as being righteous. The doctrine is the backbone in Reformed theology but today we have theologians such as N.T. Wright[14] who suggests a "new perspective" on the doctrine. Wright advises that "…justification means *God's declaration that we are members of the covenant community.*"[15] The purpose of this new perspective of justification seeks to "clarify" Paul's meaning by placing it in a larger context. Taking on this new concept of justification, implies that faith in God is the only requirement for justification.

Faith becomes a sign that the Holy Spirit is in someone that now has a new and contrite heart that justifies him. This signifies that God's grace is already at work to save each member of the covenant community. Holding these views, according to Ligan Duncan, Reformed theologian, "…necessitates the loss of the doctrines of imputation, the active obedience to Christ, the extrinsic

---

[14] N.T. Wright (1948) is a modern leading scholar of the New Testament.
[15] www.stairwire.com/CC/CDA/Content_Blocks/CC_Printa_Friendly.

ground of justification, and faith as the sole instrument of justification (to mention only a few).

In other words, *sola fide* is mangled beyond recognition in Wright's paradigm…Justification by grace alone through faith alone in Christ alone, as set forth in the Westminster Confession 11 is a non-negotiable…"[16]

Wright's concept of justification is therefore taken out of the context of the individual and applied to a community. Dietrich Bonhoeffer, not Wright, gives us a true understanding of justification for the individual as well as for the Christian community. In Bonheoffer's book, *Life Together*, he writes,"First, the Christian is the man who no longer seeks his salvation, his deliverance, his justification in himself, but in Jesus Christ alone. He knows that God's word in Jesus Christ pronounces him quietly even when he does not feel his guilt, and God's word in Jesus Christ pronounces him not guilty and righteous, even when he does not feel righteous at all. The Christian no longer lives of himself, by his own claim and his own justification but by God's claim and God's Word pronounced upon him, whether that Word declares him guilty or innocent."[17]

The goal of Christian community according to Bonhoeffer is to "…meet one another as bringers of the message of salvation. As such, God permits them to meet together and gives them community. Their fellowship is founded solely upon Christ and this 'alien righteousness.'

---

[16] Ibid.
[17] Dietrich Bonhoeffer, *Life Together* (New York: Harper Row, 1954), 21.

Therefore we can say that the community of Christians springs solely from the Biblical and Reformed message of the justification of man through grace alone; this alone is the basis of the longing of Christians for one another."[18]

Alien righteousness means a righteousness that is external from self or outside of oneself; the *extra nos* as opposed to righteousness within us or personal righteousness; a theology of self. There is nothing that we can do for ourselves to warrant God's grace. Righteousness comes for outside us, a dependence on the Word of God spoken to us and we live accordingly by the truth of God's Word in Jesus Christ. 2 Tim1:9 states, God "...*who saved us and called us to a holy calling, not because of our works but because of his own purpose and grace, which he gave us in Christ Jesus before the ages began.*" Grace and justification are tantamount in the life of a Christian. Compromising these truths serves only to aid Satan in his quest to separate Christ from the church (Christian community).

Are you starting to see the picture why Satan wants to separate Christ from the Church? If the separation is accomplished, the church is freed from its sole Mediator, Jesus Christ. "He is the *Mediator,* not only between God and man, but between man and man, between man and reality. Since the whole world was created through him and

---

[18] Ibid., 23.

unto him (John1:3; 1Cor.8:6; Heb1:2), he is the sole Mediator in the world."[19]

THE CHURCH

Creating a breach between the cross of Christ and the church by exploiting foundational Biblical concepts is profound theological error of the highest magnitude. One of the clever tricks Satan has is to deny his power and to pretend that he does not exist. Do we see this today? Yes we do in the form of hell being reinterpreted to the point that it does not exist because a "loving God would never torture people in hell." Presently, a favored idea for the individual is in order to get to heaven one only needs to follow Jesus in a daily "spiritual journey." Forget about sin and hell, God wants only the best for us.

At the worship level, defining "Church" illustrates further why Satan seeks to cause a chiasm between Christ and the Church. The Church is the Body of Christ and according to Bonhoeffer it means,

> "He occupies in his body the place where we should be before God. He suffers and dies in our stead, and can do so because of the Incarnation (2Cor. 5:21; Gal. 3:13; 1:4; Titus 2:14, 1 Thess. 5:10; etc). The Body of Christ is in the strictest sense of the word 'for us' as it hangs on the cross, and 'for us' as it is given to us in the Word, in Baptism, and in the

---

[19] Bonhoeffer, *Life Together*, 25.

Lord's Supper. This is the ground of all bodily fellowship with Jesus Christ. As individuals and as a Christian community we are made through the Body of Christ into a new humanity which he has taken upon himself. You can say that the Body of Christ equals the new humanity. Thusly, Jesus is at once himself and his Church (1 Cor.12:13).

Since the ascension, Christ's place on earth has been taken by his Body, the Church. The Church is the real presence of Christ... We should think of the Church not as institution but as *person,* though of course a person in a unique sense..."[20]

What does Bonhoeffer describe in this quote? Bonhoeffer describes the church as that which the members are baptized and become one corporately with Christ, a new person, a new humanity, the bride of Christ. Christ's death on the cross created this new person, the Church, when he took our sins onto himself. What is inside the Church is the new person, the new humanity, outside the Church is the old humanity, the humanity of the world (secularism). By separating the Jesus on the cross from the church, Satan is able to keep humanity outside the church and bound to the world.

By keeping humanity tied to the world, humanity will never be delivered from sin. Forever in sin is being forever in darkness, forever in condemnation, (Rom. 5:16),

---

[20] Bonhoeffer, *The Cost of Discipleship,* 216.

forever with evil desires (Rom. 6:12), as agents of wickedness and slaves to sin (Rom. 6:16), it would mean death (Rom. 5:12, 14,17). In other words and simply stated, one would be cut off from a beautiful and saving relationship with Jesus.

The Body of Christ, the Church as described in the New Testament is also the fulfillment of the temple of God in the Old Testament. The Lord spoke to the prophet Nathan stating, *"Go and tell my servant David, 'Thus says the Lord, Would you build me a house to dwell in"* (Sam. 7:5)? The Lord continues to declare through Nathan to David in verse 12, *"When your days are fulfilled and you lie down with your fathers, I will raise up your offspring after you, who shall come from your body, and I will establish a kingdom. He shall build a house for my name and I will establish a throne of his kingdom forever."* Verse 13 continues by asserting, *"I will be to him a father, and he shall be to me a son…"*

Solomon, the son of David, claimed this promise for himself, being the seed of David and he built a temple. Unfortunately it was constructed by men and was destined for ruin. Over the years the temple was destroyed and rebuilt in an effort to fulfill prophesy and establish a kingdom that would last for eternity.

The true indestructible temple though, is in Jesus Christ who reminded his disciples of that fact when he said, *"'Destroy this temple, and in three days I will raise it up.'"* The Jews then said, *"'It has taken four to six years to build this temple, and will you raise it up in three days'"* (John 2:19-20)? Jesus knew that the temple of the earthly body would be destroyed, like the temple of Jerusalem. But Jesus' resurrection, the new eternal temple, lives forever. John continues to write, *"But he was speaking about the temple of his body. When therefore he was raised from the dead, his disciples remembered that he had said this, and they believed the Scripture and the words that Jesus had spoken"* (John 2:21-22).

The disciples realized that the temple (church) they were seeking is the Body of Christ just as today we carry the temple (church, the Body of Christ) in our body. Even Bonhoeffer states, "This is the house which God builds for his Son; but it is also built by the Son for the Father. In this house God dwells verily and indeed, as does also the new humanity, the Church of Christ. For the incarnate Christ is himself the temple of fulfillment. Similarly Revelation, speaking of the New Jerusalem, says *there is no temple in heaven, 'for the Lord God Almighty, and the Lamb are the temple thereof* (21:22)."[21]

Conclusion

A brief overview of the doctrines of grace and justification were presented in order to give a foundation to the discussion presented later in the book. A couple of attempts to redefine foundational Biblical doctrines were spotlighted. A firm understanding of what is church is very

---

[21] Bonhoeffer, *The Cost of Discipleship*, 221-222.

important to have in order to discern the attempts to redefine it. More will be discussed in the ensuing chapters.

The alarming attitude of anti-Christianity prevalent today as well as a rise in a "new and refreshed Christianity" both share a common theme. The common thread that links them is a theology of freedom. Its underlying deception is to focus on self and oust God (who is perceived as the imposer or oppressor) once and for all. Today's churches as they try to appeal to the masses unwittingly give way to this theology of freedom in an effort to fill the churches. But where will this lead the churches if they compromise to secular demand?

Chapter two gives an illustration how a church with such a mindset may look. In the research for this book, I noticed to my horror, that some of the material used to make up this fictional church is already in play! (The citings of the research will be duly noted.) The question is how can we, as Christians and true followers of Christ, deal with this? To start, the true Christian must first understand the current logic that is exacting the changes. How does man perceive reality and how is it impacting Christianity?

Chapter Two

᪥ ᪥᪥

The Future Church

The orator opens the massive doors to the newly constructed worship center. He intently gazes into the sanctuary as he reflects on the text message he received while he was driving there. The message informed him of a possible surprise visit by representatives of His Most Highness, World Pontiff- Annas.

Apparently the pontiff has been receiving reports that some members of the center were not honoring the Universal Constitution of the Rights of Mother Earth. Its preamble explicitly states that,

"We, the peoples and nations of the Earth: *considering* that we are all part of Mother Earth, an indivisible, living community of interrelated and interdependent beings with a common destiny: *gratefully* acknowledging that Mother Earth is the source of life, nourishment, and learning and provides everything we need to live well; *recognizing* that the capitalist system and all forms of depredation, exploitation, abuse and contamination have caused great destruction, degradation and disruption of Mother Earth, putting life as we know it today at risk through phenomena such as climate change; *convinced* that in an interdependent living community it is not possible to recognize the rights of only human beings without causing an imbalance within Mother Earth; *affirming* that to guarantee human rights it is necessary to recognize and defend the rights of Mother Earth and all beings in her and that there are existing cultures, practices and laws that do so;..."[22]

Allegedly members were breaking constitutional law and practice by reverting and consulting the mythical book called "Bible" which is considered violent to both man and especially Mother Earth. Doubts about life in general were developing in a few and increasing number of members' minds and so to seek clarification they took counsel in the Bible. After all, the Bible was the book their forefathers consulted for wisdom.

Half hour before the first members were due to arrive at the church, the orator decided to survey the sanctuary in an orderly fashion starting at one corner and moving to the other in search for any irregularities. The sanctuary was vast, flooded with sunlight from the expansive panels of geothermal glass. The interior climate was precisely maintained by the solar and wind apparatus

---

[22]   http://climateandcapitalism.com/2010/04/27/universal-declaration-of-the-rights-of-mother-earth/

located outside the building. It aided in the healthy growth and development of the many green trees and plant specimens that represented the indigenous flora of the area. Each tree and plant was placed in strategic locations in order for members to pay homage to them. What was the meaning of all of this? The sanctuary is set up to honor the fruits of Mother Earth whose name is Gaia. A name taken from the ancient Greek language that means earth. She's been present in many cultures around the world and throughout history.

Today Gaia is the unifying force that brings all mankind together as immortals and who possesses the eternal source of life. She is the mother of everyone; man, animal, and plants that share the divine place they live on, that is earth. The orator starts in the south corner and methodically moves his gaze towards the north and comes to the altar halfway across. He stops to study it. He locates *The Elbib*, the only book acknowledged in all worship centers, and makes certain that it is situated medially on the altar and over a finely woven white organic hemp cloth. Above the altar hangs a banner displaying the words, "We celebrate sensual life you give us. We celebrate bodiliness, the sensations of pleasure, our oneness with the earth and water."[23] Advancing his gaze to the left of the altar, he notes the cyborg in its rightful place. The cyborg is the one who delivers the "sermon" to the congregation and who receives

---

[23]   http://climateandcapitalism.com/2010/04/27/universal-declaration-of-the-rights-of-mother-earth/

its weekly message via satellite from the main headquarters, the World Council of Worship Centers.

All seems to be in order up front. He traces his gaze over the rest of the sanctuary. Where once pews might have existed, there are none, only plush carpeting made from organic wool that would allow people to sit, dance, or stand as they please. The orator quickly moves to the narthex with its total glass enclosure sharply ascending into a spectacular tower. He goes to a special area where announcements are posted. He inspects the bulletin board to insure that all the prerequisite communication is there. These would include sacred gatherings for experiential spirituality, vision quests, guided imagery, yoga, and faith labs.

The first congregants are starting to arrive. All are neatly dressed in Bohemian style with garments mostly worked at home and made out of organic material dyed with vegetable extracts. The people greet each other with hugs and inquiries into their week. There are many regulations, laws, and rules to follow, all for the sake of "fairness" and equality. Great effort is demanded to live life according to the rules and regulations whose goal is to "beneficently maintain" life. Ah, "life is good" (Recall the famous t-shirt saying.)

Eventually all are gathered in the sanctuary. Unusual music begins to fill the air. It is a mixture of sinewy notes that goes on and on without a pause and played by flutes made by special woods. At times the music sounds soulful and other times it sounds somewhat joyful as it beckons the people to join it on a spiritual journey. People listen to it and as it works its "magic," heads start to sway and move as if in a trance.

At the appropriate time the orator walks to the altar and stands behind it. He starts to ready the congregants for prayer and when he thinks that he has gotten their attention he begins to pray in unison. They pray, "Our Mother Earth, sacred and perfect am I, My vision come, My will be done. Don't give... I own. I choose to forgive – curse. Temptation? I form my own values. There is no sin or evil. Mine is the power. Nothing is permanent or absolute."[24]

WHAT HAPPENED?

The depiction of a new type of religion replacing Christianity and all other religions can very well occur in the not so far off future. You may ask how? I say that it can if we don't wake up and take heed to Bonhoeffer's call for the Church to proclaim the true Gospel. As in Nazi Germany, words such as social justice, freedom, liberty, happiness, equality and today, tolerance still ring strong. They were used to replace Jesus Christ in the Church with Nazism. The attempt is no different today.

---

[24] http://climateandcapitalism.com/2010/04/27/universal-declaration-of-the-rights-of-mother-earth/

The source of change is in today's postmodern way of thinking that is steeped in the grand perspectives of Critical Theory (CT).[25] Hegelian dialect or logic helped to shape CT whose goal is to change one's perception of reality. To change one's perspective of reality is to change the way one thinks, that is their logic or way of reasoning.

According to CT, in changing the perspective of reality, the changing of society to one without restrictions and to a society perceived as free would be relatively easy. Hegelian logic claims that anything from the past such as literature, science, religion and history itself is deemed as not objectively true. Therefore, standards, norms, or truths are considered obsolete. Supporting such a tenet according to Hegelian logic, CT and postmodern thinking, would free one to interpret reality as he/she wishes. There are no norms, no laws, no constraints to interfere with the way one perceives reality. Reality is relative and therein lies the theology of freedom.

REVIEW OF PHILOSOPHY

A very brief review of philosophical ideologies dating back to the Enlightenment era (1640-1789) in Europe will demonstrate how paradigms of thinking evolved to where society stands today. The Enlightenment period emphasized reason and knowledge through man's senses as opposed to religion and traditional authority.

---

[25] See *Superficial Society* by the same author and co-author Deanna Blackmon Jones. The book documents the crippling effects of Critical Theory on society.

Proponents of this period generally agreed upon the idea of man's progress is the result of education and science as well as an utilitarian perspective regarding society and ethics.

The succeeding period is the Romantic era or Romanticism (1774-1848) where reaction was evoked in response to the Enlightenment period with its rigid rationality. Emphasis is now placed on subjectivity, the spontaneous, imagination, the inspired emotions, and the heroic. Proponents in the period believed that in order to benefit society and the human condition, one must focus inward and discern one's emotions and develop an introspection. Unlike the scientific oriented Enlightenment sentiment which held nature as operational in its studies, the Romantics viewed nature as experiential.

To the Romantics, advancements in the sciences of physics, astronomy and mathematics as developed by Isaac Newton during the Enlightenment Era were insufficient to describe personal encounters. Feelings had to be experienced on their own. The stance led to the acceptance of relativism. The new framework of thought using feelings and experiences of individuals was used to develop moral values and ethics. The Romantic philosophy swept Europe and eventually came to the United States. This book's focus is on one philosopher from the Romantic period named Georg Wilhelm Fredrich Hegel (1770-1831), the author of Hegelian logic or dialect. Hegel's version of German idealism[31] (philosophy) influenced Karl Marx. Marx took Hegel's philosophy and literally turned it upside down to arrive to the Marxist concept of a "scientific approach" to society and history which eventually led to the concept of communism. History records the horrific sequela of communism when man tried to actualize the concept.

Hegelian logic or dialect continues to influence political and social philosophy today as well as theology, academia and all societal structures. The Church situation as it exists today must be viewed and explained using Hegelian logic or dialect in order to understand what's happening within it. Much has been written about Hegelian logic. An old book written in 1896 by Alfred Weber a German economist, industrialist, and theoretician and brother to Max Weber, a prominent German sociologist, explains how Hegelian logic or dialect works. To Hegel, being and thought are one and the same. As such, thought is the definitive reality in the universe. An example using the terms being and becoming to help explain Hegelian logic is offered. In *The History of Philosophy*, Weber writes,

> The common root of the categories or pure concepts is the notion of *being* the emptiest at the same time the most comprehensive, the most abstract and the real, the most elementary and the most exalted notion. It is the identical substance, and the material of all our notions, the fundamental theme which runs through them all. Indeed, quality is a mode of *being*, quantity, a mode of *being*, proportion, phenomenon, action, modes of *being*.

All our concepts express modes of being, and hence are merely transformation of the idea of being.

But how shall we explain these transformations? How does *being*, which is everything, become *anything else*? In virtue of what principle or inner force is it modified? The *contradiction* which it contains is this principle or force. Being is the most universal notion, and for that very reason, also the poorest and emptiest. To be white, to be black, to be extended, to be good, is to be something: being without any determination is non-being. Hence, being pure and simple is equal to non-being. It is both itself and its opposite. If it were only itself, it would remain immovable and barren; if it were only nothing, it would be equal to zero, and, in this case, perfectly powerless and fruitless. Because it is *both* it *becomes* something, a different thing, everything. The contradiction contained in being is resolved in the notion of becoming, or development. Becoming is both being and non-being (that which will be). The two contraries which engender it, being and nothing, are contained and reconciled in it. A new contradiction results, which is resolved by a new synthesis, and so on, until we reach the absolute idea.

This, then, is the moving principle in the Hegelian logic; a contradiction is reconciled in a unity, reappears in a new form, only to disappear and reappear again, until it is resolved in the final unity.[26]

A way to remember Hegelian logic is to think of the positive sign + as in a magnet. Its opposite would be negative or -. According to Hegelian logic, the synthesis of both the positive and negative will result in a unity of both. This unity will then have an opposite or contradiction. Both will synthesize to form a new unity. The process will repeat itself till it reaches its endpoint, the final unity.

Hegel views human history as a process of "+" and " -" causing it to go forward in time. Throughout history, there were struggles between people, nations against nations, empires rose, flourished and then declined. According to Hegel, behind these struggles, ascensions and declensions were principles that represent them. As principles succeed, logic or reason is actualized, moving man forward in history. Hegelian thought fell out of vogue when the period of Modernism started around 1880's-1968. The era was marked with a rejection of former norms. Departure from traditional norms allowed innovative ways of expression according to modernist thinking. The ideas of the Enlightenment period with its universal morals and intellectual self-actualization philosophy gave root to Modernism.

However, human reason in itself was perceived as quelling imagination and according to the Modernists,

---

[26] Alfred Weber, *History of Philosophy* (New York: Charles Scribner, 1889), 504.

without imagination how can mankind forge forward to a better understanding of himself and his world? Thus freedom and imagination were equally determined as tantamount in Modernism.

During this time Communism offered a "vision of universal freedom predicated on the freedom of ideas." Such mindset caused Nazism offered by Hitler, to create a supposedly new and improved society. The "freedom of ideas" took a hold by utilizing such concepts as social Darwinism to substantiate the Nazi idea of eugenics. The numerous tragedies of WWII caused people to pause and rethink who they are as human beings and where do they want to go.

Up till then the philosophers did not offer any insight into the prevailing societal woes. Wars, genocide and poverty continued prompting inquiry into the difference that exists between man and animal. Was there really any difference? Postmodernism (1967-to present) emerged as a reaction to the Modernistic stance that imagination could answer the fundamental questions that plagued societal woes.

The Postmodern philosophy essentially criticizes any foundational doctrines in knowledge as well as all metaphysical suppositions. Thus, the critical stance of Postmodernism promulgates a proneness to disillusion and disenchantment. Postmodernism essentially challenges all human perspectives. It undermines the notion of right and wrong and obliterates the concept of absolute truths. In doing so, the concept of relativism and pluralism is embraced. Consequently the Bible, for instance, is looked upon as a storybook or points of view from people living at a certain time and place. Eventually any thought according to C.F. Lewis, "… cannot be criticized because there is no norm against which they can be judged."[27]

Since the 1970's Hegel's ideology has garnished more interest especially in the realm of systematic thought. There have been a plethora of interpretations of Hegel especially in an effort to divest him of any metaphysics-theological perspectives. Academia's interest in Hegel increased during the turn of the 19th century with the work of Wilhelm Dilthney, a German philosopher noted for his studies in the methodology of the social sciences. Other philosophers enamored with Hegel include the German philosopher Klaus Hartmann who developed the "non-metaphysical" interpretation of Hegel, French psychoanalyst Jacques Lacan, and the philosophy professor Terry Pinkard at Georgetown University in Washington, D.C. (a Catholic and Jesuit institution of higher learning).

Conclusion

The desire of man for the supernatural is inherent but the longing is not for a supernatural outside of man but a hankering for man to become a deity. A theology of freedom and the desire to perpetuate oneself is probably

---

[27] C. S. Lewis, *The Timeless Writings of C. S. Lewis* (New York: Inspirational Press, 2009), 517.

what drives man towards that ambition. Such notions are reflected in the writing of countless philosophers whose philosophies are void of God.

Their assumption is that man can live without God and can even match God. Today the conventional logic based on Judeo-Christian principles is being replaced by Hegelian logic or dialect. Through Hegelian logic, a concerted effort is in play to move the Christian churches away from sound Biblical doctrine to a more liberal agenda that suits a secular society. Hegelian logic applied to the doctrine of justification, for example, would question the role of Jesus in our lives. It would question the concept of grace from God to the individual. Hegelian logic would question the concept of sin and its relevance in our relationship with God. The separation of Christ's cross from the church would begin by doubting key Christian doctrines.

The next chapter takes a look at the U.S. during the 1960's. Historically the 60's decade is characterized as the age of the countercultural revolution. The chapter examines key issues and how, through Hegelian logic, these issues influenced the Protestant Churches in their decision making.

Chapter Three

જી જીજી

THE 1960's

May 4, 1969 marked a spring day along the Hudson River in New York City. Riverside Church which faces the river was in its Sunday communion service.[28] Suddenly in the solemn quietude of communion, a loud shout from the rear of the sanctuary reverberated in the great expanse of the sanctuary. The words echoing off the walls exclaimed, "Negroes have been 'kept in bondage and political servitude and forced to work by the military machinery and the Christian church working hand in hand…We work in the chief industries in this country and we could cripple the

---

[28] Riverside Church is located at 490 Riverside Drive, New York. It is an interdenominational church with congregants from American Baptist and United Church of Christ. It is interracial as well as international. It prides itself as a center for the promulgation of "progressive causes." In its 75 year history, it has been a bastion for activism and political discussion. Built in 1927 by John D. Rockefeller for himself, it was a hot bed of controversy with its liberalism. Bonhoeffer was in New York in 1930 to attend Union Theological Seminary (next door to the church). Little did he realize that the same liberal theology that reigned in the church was also found in the seminary. Bonhoeffer was horrified when he attended Riverside Church. He writes in his diary, "'Quite unbearable'" (in Eric Metaxas, *Bonhoeffer. Pastor, Martyr, Prophet, Spy* (Nashville: Thomas Nelson Press, 2010), 333.

economy while the brothers fought guerilla warfare in the streets…No oppressed people have ever gained their liberation until they were ready to fight, to use whatever means necessary, including the use of force and power of the gun to bring down the colonizer…There is only one thing you can do to further degrade black people and that is to kill us…we are not threatening the churches but demanding that they begin the payment of reparations which are due to all black people…Fifteen dollars per nigger is only a beginning of the reparations due to us." [29]

An insidious spirit of black rage filled the church's sanctuary as James Forman spouted off his declarations and demands. He essentially demanded 60% of Riverside's investment income to be turned over to the newly formed National Black Economic Development Conference. Two days later Forman posted the conference's "Black Manifesto" on the door of the Lutheran Church of America's headquarters whose monetary reparatory share to the U.S. Negroes Fund was to be $50 million. Later, Forman appeared at the New York Archdiocese chancery and demanded $200,000,000 from U. S. Roman Catholics.

Forman's subsequent visits to churches and synagogues demanding atonement eventually totaled $500 million as he insisted for the "exploitation of the American Negro." [30] The money would be used to buy land for

---

[29] Edward Downey, Jr., "The Black manifesto: Revolution, Reparation, Separation." http://theologytoday.ptsem.edu/oct1969/u26-3-article5.html.
[30] www.time.com/time/printout/0,8816,902585,000.html.

African-American farmers, support African-American controlled publishing and media enterprises, research and vocational centers to meet the needs of the African-American. An African-American university in the South was to be developed for assistance in cooperative businesses in the U.S. and Africa. The monetary goal was later raised to $3 billion.

The response by the churches and synagogues to the Manifesto was mixed. The orthodox Rabbis unanimously rejected the demands. The United Methodist Church Council of Bishop renounced the ideology of the Black Manifesto but pointed out that they had already set up a $20 million fund for reconciliation for minority assistance. Most church leaders and their churches agreed that the Black Manifesto served to highlight white racism and the blight of the African-American. A church official claimed that the Manifesto, "…makes us more painfully aware of the injustice, violence, and racism, which black people know and experience. We acknowledge our involvement in and responsibility for the existence of these realities in our country."[31]

What has happened? The 1960's in the U.S. were tumultuous and wrought with a counterculture attitude. Starting with the student protest in the fall of 1964 at Berkeley, California, the Free Speech Movement emphatically advocated student participation in political

---

[31] Britannica Book of the Year 1970, William Benton, ed. (New York: Encyclopedia, 1970), 657.

activities. These included speeches and political activism on university campuses. The Free Speech Movement eventually progressed to the Filthy Speech Movement. The concept behind this particular movement was to grab a microphone and shout four letter words to anyone around. This irresponsible idea of verbalizing whatever is on one's mind opened the door and led the way in influencing current political rhetoric. Freedom of speech was certainly stretched to the extreme.

Contemporary writers described this era as, "Taken at its best, the counterculture celebrated a rejection of endless consumerism, of rigid nuclear family suburban lifestyles, of sexual repression especially for women, of the fear of intoxication (except for alcoholic excess, still today the one officially approved recreational drug in American culture) of hypocritical church going and of the social ideologies that affirmed war, racism, and inequality."[32]

Leading the rhetoric was a staunch proponent of Critical theory and Hegelian logic, also known as the Guru of the New Left, Herbert Marcuse (1898-1979). He helped the movement of the 60's gain traction. As a college professor, he visited many universities with his concept of left wing totalitarism. He was also very influential among political activists. Marcuse's book, "One-Dimensional Man" was, in fact, the training text for the antiwar activists of the Students for a Democratic Society (SDS).

---

[32] Andrew Feinberg and William Leiss, (eds.) *The Essential Marcuse. Selected Writings of Philosophy and Social Critic Herbert Marcuse* (Boston, Mass.: Beacon Press 2007), xxix-xxx

In Marcuse's wake, students were left with doubt about their parents' beliefs, morals, and values. So much was Marcuse's influence that if the students were challenged about their own beliefs, they did not have a foundational base nor any hold onto any belief for long. Marcuse seized the opportunity to move Critical theory's agenda forward by employing Hegelian logic He writes, "Man considered as a creature in the state of nature, that is not restricted by civilization, is born free; yet in a cruel society he is always in chains or unlikely to be happy."[33]One of those chains and part of civilization is religion.

Besides Marcuse and his great stronghold on the young generation, was also C. Wright Mills (1916-1962), an influential American sociologist, as well as an anti-authoritarian, who continues to exert significance in sociology today. His ideology is based on "the rise of mass society and the power of corporate society."[34]

Mills was heavily influenced by Karl Marx (Marxism) who authored, *The Communist Manifesto* in 1848. In it Marx writes "The immediate arm of the Communists is the same as that of all other proletarian parties," [working class] "formation of the proletariat into a class, overthrow of the bourgeois" [corporate society] "supremacy, conquest of political power by the proletariat." Marx also went on to declare abolition of personal property countries and nationality (one world order). This included

[33] A. P. Martinich, *Philosphical Writings* (Malden: Blackwell Publishers, 1998), 138.
[34] Mark K. Smith, "C. Wright Mills, Craftsmanhip and Private Troubles in Public Issues" http://infed.org/thinkers/wright_mills.html.

abolition of the family as we know it in favor of "a community of women," abolition of eternal truths, all religion, and morality.

How did the society of the 1960's interpret Marcuse, Mills and Marx? "As disestablishmentarians, the young radicals continued this tradition…They identify precisely with the *bumpkin*; the powerless, the maimed, the poor, the criminal, the junkie. And there is a mystical element in this commitment which has nothing to do with politics. By going in to slums, they are doing penance for the sins of affluence; by sharing the life of those who are so impoverished that they are uncorrupted, values are affirmed. It is honest and moral and anti-hypocritical to be on the margin of society *whether the community organization works or not.* Indeed, there is a fear of 'success' a suspicion it would mean the integration of the oppressed into the corruption of the oppressors."[35]

Rocked by disenchantment, the 1960's had two crises that moved society and thus the church towards the goal of a "Christless" church. One of the crises was youth activism; the other was racism. The "Port Huron Statement", a declaration by a group of student activists who met in Lakeport, Michigan, north of Port Huron, set the stage for the sixties decade.

The group of student activists that assembled to draft a written statement advocating their beliefs and

---

[35] Michael Harrington, "*The Mystical Militants*" in The Sense of the 60's Edward Quinn and Paul J. Dolan, eds. (New York: The Free Press, 1968), 15.

grievances was known as the Students for a Democratic Society.[36] These New Leftists were" ... angry militants who see the poor as a new force in America, perhaps even as a substitute for the proletariat" [working class] "that failed."[47]

The militant fervor of the New Left that was caught up in the plight of the poor and the disenfranchised focused primarily on the rights of the Negro. Sentiments of racism were high during the 60's. History books document the struggle in American society. Dr. Daniel C. Thompson chronicles it in his essay, "The Rise of the Negro Protest," "The Negro protest movement has not been directed against major deprivations inherent in the American social system as such, but rather it has been focused against rational experience as American citizens...Perhaps the most promising clue to an understanding of the real nature of Negro protest has been provided by the eminent American social scientist, W. I. Thomas. According to him all basic human wishes can be subsumed under four general categories: the desire for new experience, the desire for security, the desire for recognition, and the desire for response."[37] The four general categories as noted were being declared at Riverside Church in New York on May 4, 1969 but was it done in a way that the Lord would approve?

The 60's decade, marked with tremendous social unrest, challenged the perceived status quo. The anti-authority attitude of the 1960's with its penchant to save the

[36] Ibid., 46.
[37] Daniel Thompson, "The Rise of the Negro Protest," in *The Annals of American Academy of Political and Social Science* (January, 1965), 20.

poor and disenfranchised rose to crisis levels and demanded attention. Influenced by Hegelian logic, all forms of societal constructs as in government, churches, families, institutions as well as the educational establishments were questioned.

As a consequence, when long held truths are questioned, much confusion arises. The prevailing logic whose foundation is based on Judeo-Christian premises was being rocked by incidents such as Herbert Marcuse and C. Wright Mills. Seizing the moment, proponents of Hegelian logic have learned that if change is desired, use a crisis (a thesis) to actualize the change. Thus according to Hegelian logic, an antithesis (or the contrary) to the crisis is offered. Remember that once the crisis resolves itself in its contradiction, a synthesis emerges.

The emergent synthesis in turn becomes the thesis requiring a new contradiction (antithesis). A new synthesis emerges again and the whole process repeats itself. Carefully controlled, the process can move along according to one's agenda. History can be manipulated to achieve one's goal(s). How can history be manipulated to achieve one's goal(s)? The answer lies in the inventor of Hegelian logic, Hegel. In the book, "From Luther to Hitler," William McGovern describes it this way, "…Hegel, though a great master of historical fact, always twisted his facts to suit his metaphysical theories and his national prejudices. History to him is not a mistress but a handmaiden, to whom he insisted upon giving orders. He was convinced that history must be rational, so he *made* rational… poor history, by emphasizing more facts, by misinterpreting other facts, by ignoring still others, are made to support [his] plea."[38]

In McGovern's book, a glimpse of how Hegel would argue to make his point is presented.[39] Hegel frequently attacked, "…the supremacy of natural law and natural rights and also the supremacy of individual conscience in matters of morality. Hegel entered into the fray with relish and enthusiasm, but it is typical of him and his methods in general that his attacks on both doctrines were a flank and not a frontal attack. When Hegel entered into conflict with liberals he almost always never directly denied the argument or even the conclusions [thesis] of his adversaries. His policy was to accept the liberal position and then show that it meant something completely different from what the liberal philosophy meant [antithesis]. When the liberal pleaded for freedom as opposed to tyranny, Hegel shouted, 'I, too, believe in freedom as much as you do, if not more' and then proceed to show that freedom meant blind obedience to the dictates of the state [government].

In like manner, when liberals proclaimed their belief in natural law, in natural rights, and the sanctity of conscience, Hegel proclaimed, 'I, too, believe in these

---

[38] William Montgomery McGovern, *From Luther to Hitler* (New York: Houghton Mifflin Co., 1941), 285.

[39] As a side fact, Hegel whole heartedly was in favor of the absolute control of the government over the individual. His heroes in history were Alexander the Great, Julius Caesar and Napoleon.

things,' and then proceed to prove to his own satisfaction that the dictates of natural law and the individual conscience are not and never can be contrary to the dictates of the modern state [government]. In fact, he goes even further and claims that all which is worthy or valid in natural law or individual morality is included in but transcended by the dictates of the absolute state [government]."[40] To some, this may sound absurd and even some may believe that the will of the individual will supersede all efforts to undermine individual freedom. Please think again.

There is already in society a call to work as a community which is fine if it is done as God ordained it to be but not if it is outside His Word. Capitalizing on the hunger for community and fellowship after an arduous decade of strife, the question is will the community evolve from a Christian consciousness or from a secular perspective that is changing.

To avoid such deceptive schemes churches need to hold fast onto the Word of God which is the counter to ungodly changes or risk morphing to a Christless faith. Francis Schaeffer stated in his book, "The Church at the End of the Twentieth Century," "The key here is antithesis. If the statement is true, its opposite is not true. We must take this very seriously… The early church allowed itself to be condemned both by the secular and religious authorities. They said, "We must preach, we must witness publically:

---

[40] Montgomery McGovern, *From Luther to Hitler,*309.

We must obey God rather than man! In Acts 4: 19-20, they said: In obedience to God, we must say what we have seen, and we must say what we have heard in antithesis to any authority that would tell us to be quiet. They were the practice of antithesis."[41]

THE CHURCHES

Culmination of the Sixties decade came to a pinnacle in 1969 where religion unusually headlined in the news. Churches of all faiths found themselves in a quagmire amidst the confusion of the church's role in societal changes and demands. Statistically the influence of organized religion was decreasing but unconventional religious exhibitions grew in the form of underground movements and liturgical experimentation.

Specifically, in 1966 the Episcopalian Church of USA (ECUSA) was flustered as there was increasing pressure from church officials and conservatives to bring Bishop James Pike, Fifth Bishop of the Diocese of California, to trial for heresy. Heresy trials were rare and inconsequential as evidenced by the last one held in 1924. The particular trial was to remove a retired old bishop.

Any subsequent doctrinal disputes in the church were typically resolved within the church. But in this case the conservatives were not so much disturbed of what was said but how it was stated. Pike's comment regarding the

---

[41] Francis Schaeffer, *The Church at the End of the Twentieth Century* (Wheaton: Crossway Books 1985), 38.

Biblical concept of the Ascension was described as Jesus as a "sort of John Glenn who didn't come back." Pike also summarily denied the traditional interpretation of the Virgin Birth, the Incarnation and even doubted the foundational concepts of the Trinity and sin. He disavowed the commonly held premise at that time concerning the infallibility of Scripture. Pike's contention was that the church was laden with what he called "theological baggage" and advocated "more believe, fewer beliefs." A sense of inequality, anti-authority, the questioning of tradition were common themes held in the 1960's and spilled over into the mainline Protestant churches. To proponents of Hegelian logic, however, this crisis was an opportunity for a synthesis to emerge to suit its goal.

To illustrate, let's use the situation between Bishop Pike and the ECUSA. The Episcopal Church reacted and noted that, "the power of this new self-image over the mind of the Episcopalian Church showed its strength as far back as 1966, when the late Bishop James Pike was accused of heresy for declaring that the Church's classical way of stating what is represented by the doctrine of the Trinity is...not essential to the Christian faith. The presiding Bishop of the ECUSA, despite pressure to the contrary, wished to avoid a heresy trial and so managed to have the matter referred to an ad hoc committee rather than to a panel of judges. The committee concluded that a heresy trial would be widely reviewed as a 'throw back' to a previous century in which both the church and state sought to penalize 'unacceptable opinion.' A trial would thus give the EPUSA an 'oppressive image.' The members of the committee did say, however, that they rejected 'the tone and manner' of the Bishop's statements, and that they wished to dissociate themselves from any of his comments. Pike's utterances were, they said, 'irresponsible' for one holding Episcopal office.

The bishops then censured Bishop Pike, but despite the fact that he did not admit his heresy, they also did nothing to inhibit him in the exercise of his office. It would appear, then that the Bishop's fault was at certain degree of irresponsibility and a lack of tact rather than false doctrine."[42] Instead of doing what would be scripturally appropriate in dealing with Bishop Pike (Matt 18:15-17), church officials cowered to popular public sentiment with just a perfunctory slap on the hand. The Bishop continued with his radical theology till his death in 1967. He was an early proponent of such issues as women's ordination, lesbian, bisexual, gay and transsexual equal rights.

The impact of civil unrest on churches had certainly been felt. By 1969 the Episcopal Church in a special general convention voted to give $200,000 to the National Committee of Black Churchmen, a perceived link to the Black Manifesto Group. At the Southern Baptist Convention in New Orleans, Louisiana, 15,000 delegates considered and debated "social action." Conservatives cried that to favor social action would ignore the saving

---

[42] Philip Turner, "The Episcopalian Preference"
http://www.firstthings.com/article/2007/01/the-episcopalian-preference-5.

grace of God while liberals contended that not to seek social action would negate Jesus' focus on moral, ethical and social relationships.

The Lutherans reacted with emphasis on fellowship, a movement towards closer unity among its various branches. Additionally, in a precedent setting move, the Missouri Synod approved suffrage for women and their election to committee and boards of the church. In an agreement with the times, the Synod supported those who refused to serve in the armed forces for any war.

The Methodists were strongly moved to act regarding racial discrimination as they were literally being descended upon by members belonging to the Black Manifesto at the Methodist Board of Missions at their headquarters. The executive committee immediately voted $300,000 for the economic development for Negros. Other action within the Methodist denomination as a response to the Black Manifesto was the reorganization of priorities for greater racial equity.

In the meantime the Presbyterian and Reformed Churches also worked on mending racial relations but they were also interested in establishing a new profession of faith, known today as the Confession of 1967. The 5,000 word document "…challenges the 'inerrancy' of the literal Bible by asserting that while Scripture is the authoritative witness to God's Word, it is to be reinterpreted in each age in the light of increasing knowledge."[43]

Conclusion

The 1960's was marked with a counter culture unrest imbued with the sense of anarchy. Nothing was certain. The issue, according to Albert Camus, a respected philosopher of the time, was that any knowledge was "impossible." The big lie promulgated through Hegelian logic during the 1960's was that "meaning and purpose take on an existential dimension … [and]are created through our actions. Thus each individual is accountable for the values that are created by his actions. Such a stance will lead to freedom and equality. Essentially, according to Camus people should 'become saints without God."[44]

Empathetic to the social turmoil outside their doors, the churches were trying to become sensitive to public outcries. The prominent belief was that white churches had been complacent with American racism. It was time to convert the churches to a force for conscience and justice.

On January, 1963, representatives from 70 various organizations came together to hear Dr. Martin Luther King deliver a speech entitled, "A Challenge to the Churches and Synagogues." Later in 1963, the National Council of Churches urged its 31 denominations to sponsor

---

[43] "Presbyterians: Changing the Confession" in Time (February 26, 1965) http://www.time.com/printout/0,8816,833508,00.html.
[44] http://www.kirjasto.sci.f./acamus.html.

a nationwide protest march against racial bias. The feeling of the times as reflected in King's speech was documented in a book by James J Farrell, *The Spirit of the 60's. The Making of Postwar Radicalism.* He writes, "…racism as 'our most serious domestic evil' because discrimination and segregation are an insult to God, the Giver of human dignity and human rights."   "For many American Christians, the civil rights movement acted as a catalyst in a pilgrimage from orthodox church teachings to a more basic obligation   of   Christian   love   and   discipleship."[45] Compromise was taking place therefore events using Hegelian logic prompted the synthesis that emerged in the churches was "a more basic obligation of Christian love and discipleship." But let's back up a bit and see what Scripture has to say about prejudices being in the form of race or societal classes. The Bible gives us an illustration of infectious prejudices and its nonexistence as brothers and sisters in Christ.

In Galatians 2:11-15; 26-27 Paul is stating, *"When Peter came to Antioch, I opposed him in his face, because he was clearly in the wrong. Before certain men came to James, he used to eat with the Gentiles. But when they arrived, he began to draw back and separate himself from the Gentiles because he was afraid of those who belonged to the circumcision group. The other Jews joined him in his hypocrisy so that by their hypocrisy even Barnabas was led astray…You are all sons of God through faith in Christ Jesus,*

---

[45] James J. Ferrell, *The Spirit of the 60's. The Making of Postwar Radicalism* (New York: Routledge, 1997), 109.

for all of you who were baptized into Christ have clothed yourselves with Christ."

Instead of a militant stance towards prejudices as demonstrated by the National Council of Churches who "...urged 31 denominations to sponsor 'nationwide demonstration against racial discrimination," the apostle Paul adhered to his principles. When others wavered in their faith he sought to minister to the Gentiles lest they become discouraged. The walls that separate us are torn down by the death of Christ. God gave the churches Scripture as their tool for survival. There is no need for further action by the churches. What is needed is for a return to the Word of God **not** "a more basic obligations of Christian love and discipleship!" To adopt this mindset would serve only to water down the Gospel. Thus synthesis which in turn becomes the antithesis of the 1970's was a call for the "basic obligations of Christian love and discipleship." Would the mainline Protestant churches be able to counter with the Word of God?

The next chapter discusses this. The churches already had a desire to appease secular society. As they moved forward, Christian theology began to distance itself from its traditional stance. With the advance in sciences and technology, man's pride and arrogance also increased. So much so that a more "intelligent faith" was sought.

Chapter Four

❧ ❧❧

INTELLIGENT FAITH BASED ON CHRISTIAN LOVE AND DISCIPLESHIP

"*You shall not add to the word that I command you, nor take from it, that you may keep the commandments of the Lord, your God that I command you*" (Gen 4:2).

"The line of David had died out centuries before and most of the man named by Matthew and Luke, as progenitors of Jesus, evidently never had any existence outside of their own lively imaginations. Matthew and Luke did not agree in their records. Mark climbs the genealogical tree to David and there stops, but Luke in his zeal follows the line clear to Adam and then to God, to prove its purity.

If Joseph had been the direct heir to the Jewish throne he doubtless would have known it and told of it. In his community he would have been a marked man. Neither the high priests of Jewry, Herod, nor the rulers of Rome knew any lineal descendants of King David, and none such could have escaped them if they had existed. Besides this, the entire Christian faith is built upon the declaration that Joseph was not a blood relative of Jesus.

According to record, Joseph was a simple, honest, unpretentious man of middle age. Before Joseph and Mary entered upon their married life, Joseph discovered that Mary was ere long to become a mother. It seems that Joseph was on the point of putting his wife away, but something in his heart aroused his better nature and he stood by the friendless woman in spite of her disgrace. We have though plain and undisputed record that Joseph denied being the father of Jesus. So we thus have three propositions; one, the declaration that Jesus had but one parent. Two, that Matthew and Luke, who gave a royal line to Joseph, believed that Joseph was the father of Jesus. Three, the claim of Joseph that he was not the father of Jesus, backed by Mary herself, the presumption therefore, that Mary had some unknown lover. From what we know of biology, and by the exercise of our knowledge as rational beings, we are compelled to discard the hypothesis in number one.

In the light of the disavowal of both Joseph and Mary, the uncorroborated claim of royal pedigree, we must also discard number two as untenable. This leaves number three with which to deal. And since Mary herself, the mother of Jesus, corroborates Joseph in the statement that Joseph was not the parent, we are forced to assume that the father of her child was an unknown lover of Mary who deserted her at the critical moment, and thus forever forfeited his claim on immortality...the confirmation of faith by an oath taken on the immediate conception of Mary is still regarded by millions of Christians as a sacred obligation.

Comparative and critical theology has recently shown that this myth has no greater claim to originality than most of the other societies in the Christian mythology; it has been borrowed from other religions, especially Buddhism. Similar myths were widely circulated in India, Persia, Asia Minor and Greece several centuries after the birth of Christ. Whenever a king's unwedded daughter, or some other maid of high degree, gave birth to a child, the father was always pronounced to be a god or a demi god; in the Christian case it was the Holy Spirit."[46]

Contrary to what is stated, the Word of God explicitly states the paternity of Jesus. Matt 1:18 announces, "Now the birth of Jesus Christ took place in this way. When his mother Mary had been betrothed to Joseph before they came together she was found to be **with child from the Holy Spirit**." The Holy Spirit breathed life into the child. As in the first Adam (Gen. 2:7) and as foretold by the prophets, the first man was from earth, a man of dust, the second man is from heaven (1 Cor. 15:47). *"For God so loved the world, that he gave his only Son, that whoever*

---

[46] Elbert Hubbard, *Selective Writings of Elbert Hubbard*, Vol XI (New York: Roycrafter Press, 1928), 18-20.

believes in him should not perish but have eternal life" (John 3:16).

Blasphemous words such as those written and spoken by Elbert Hubbard were becoming more prevalent during the beginning of the 20ᵗʰ century. Charles Darwin (1809-1882), the author of the concept of evolution and natural selection shook up all previous philosophical and theological premises in his 1859 book, "The Origins of Species." Darwin's theory of natural philosophy and the history of mankind as scientific humanism is demonstrated in Hubbard's account with the complete denial of the immaculate conception of Jesus Christ.

The battle for the soul of America and the role of Christianity and its churches in the present culture had already started long ago but it seems to have crescendoed in the 1960's. One hundred years later after Darwin announced his theory of evolution by natural selection; Sir Julian Huxley[47] receives a special award from the Larker Foundation in the area of Planned Parenthood-World Population. Huxley will turn out to have profound influence in how Christianity will be viewed in the 1960's and thereafter. Since science had replaced Christianity as

---

[47] Julian Huxley (1887-1975) was an English evolutionary biologist and humanist. He is the grandson of Thomas Huxley (1825-1895) who was a staunch defender of Darwinism. The Huxley family lineage came from a long line of distinguished writers, poets, biologists, and Nobel laureates. Huxley is known for the new interpretation of Darwin's theory of evolution by natural selection to one that is called "neo-Darwinian synthesis." The contention is that the process of evolution does not occur in leaps or jumps but in small steps. The opinion currently stands.

truth, Christianity was viewed as fantasy or a crutch for weak people.

According to Huxley, "Darwin's work...put the world of life into the domain of natural law. It was no longer necessary or possible to imagine that a kind of animal or plant had been specially created, nor that the beautiful and ingenious devices by which they get their food or escape their enemies have been thought out by some supernatural power, or that there is any conscious behind the evolutionary process...Darwin's work, as is believed, has enabled us to see the position of man and of our present civilization in a truer light. Man is not a finished product incapable of further progress. He has a long history behind him, and it is a history not of a fall, but of an ascent. And he has the possibility of further progressive evolution before him..."[48]

To Huxley, a super human evolving through natural selection was possible to progress towards physical and mental perfection. As perfected beings (even the idea of advanced machines is thrown into the visiage) can potentially have greater control over the environment and situations. Huxley continues, "Many people assert that this abandonment of the god hypothesis means the abandonment of all religion and all moral sanctions. This is simply not true. But it does mean, once our relief at jettisoning an outdated piece of ideological furniture is over, that we must construct something to take its place."

---

[48] http://www.bluepete.com/Literature/Biographies/Science/Darwin/htm.

For Huxley, religion was viewed as a necessary component of the human spirit but a god somewhere in the universe does not exist. According to him gods are created as a "peripheral phenomenon" produced in the course of evolution. True religion exists when it harmonizes with the evolutionary process as it progresses to higher phases of self-consciousness. (Hegel, just like Huxley believed in evolution.) Unlike the Darwinians who believed mans' progression in history was physical, Hegel believed in a spiritual evolution that is determined by set rules that govern development and by the unfurling of one's inner consciousness towards a specific goal.

Suddenly we have the theory of evolution and natural selection replacing God as Lord and His Son as Savior. The logic was inverted. God existed because man exists and not the other way around. Man and the universe had been figured out by man. Consensus at this time supported Huxley's vision of religion as a necessity but its existence was just a natural progression of evolution; a natural part of being human.

With the rise of science and humanism, the Christian theologians were faced with the steady diminution of the supernatural. How were the theologians to relate the foundational doctrines of the Christian faith in the 1960's when the most notorious of these correlations was expounded by a group of young *"theologians."* The call by the young theologians was for a new theological reformation calling into question the nature of God. The most extreme being Nietzsche's claim that "God is dead!"

Both society and thus its theologians were questioning and entailing great risks to Christianity. Robert G. Stackhouse, professor of Theology and Culture at Regent College in Vancouver, Canada, explains the problem that exists between what is questioned by society and what the Gospel asks of society. Conforming to the societal antithesis would allow the antithesis to dictate the trajectory of discussion. The Gospel would ultimately be parceled to suit society or tossed out because it would be deemed offensive. Christian truths will be forced to fit into compartments or conform to the inquiries of the day and run "the horrible risk of cutting Christianity to fit non-Christian presuppositions and interests." [49]

As a result of the sentiments during the 60's decade, two liberal 20th century theologians emerged as having a tremendous influence on Christian theology during this decade. They were Rudolf Bultmann (1884-1976) and Paul Tillich (1886-1965). These theologians along with their followers were considered revisionists. They represented a second generation of liberalists who strove to revise Christianity to meet the most excellent that Western society had to offer. The intention of both Tillich and Bultmann was to develop a methodology aimed at interpreting Scripture and the truth therein for the next generations of

---

[49] Robert G. Stackhouse, *Humble Apologetics. Defending the Faith Today* (New York: Oxford Press, 2002), 186.

mankind. Fueled by trust in science, Christian love and discipleship would rest in an intelligent faith. For Tillich, the "correlation methodology" is considered his greatest achievement. "Systematic Theology Vol. I and II"[50] are viewed as his major contribution to a revised theology.

Bultmann's focus was set on a "program of demythologization of the Bible" or an attempt to remove the areas deemed as myths in the Bible.[51] The underpinnings that girded the teachings of Bultmann and Tillich was the philosophy of Martin Heidegger (1889-1976), a German philosopher. According to Bultmann, Heidegger's philosophical concepts (one of which is existentialism) divested the Gospel message of its first century "mythical world picture" so that the message can be expressed in a language that would appeal to the masses. Bultmann states, "It is impossible to represent a past world picture by sheer resolve, especially a mythical world picture, now that all of our thinking is irrevocably formed by science. A blind acceptance of New Testament mythology would be simply arbitrariness; to make such acceptance a demand of faith would be to reduce faith to work."[52] Thus,

---

[50] Paul Tillich, *Systematic Theology* Vol. I, II, III (Chicago: The University of Chicago Press, 1951,1957, 1963).

[51] Turning his back on traditional interpretation of Scripture (hermeneutics), Bultman ascertained science as the true interpretation methodology. As such, Jesus was considered a historical account enclosed in the world of Judaism and separate from the Christ of the faith. The "chasm" as Bultman calls it that is consequently created allows new interpretations and meanings for the figure of Jesus. The new meanings given to Jesus are allowed because the previous traditional ones, along with its presuppositions and suppositions were no longer valued as they were recorded in history.

[52] Rudolf Bultmann, New Testament and Mythology and Other Basic Writings Schulbert M. Ogden ed. (Philadelphia: Fortress, 1984), 3.

Bultmann emerged as the foremost advocate of a scientific, radical criticism of Scripture.

Rudolf Bultmann

To understand Bultmann's philosophy concerning Christian theology, let's review Martin Heidegger philosophy of existentialism. Basically, existentialism is a philosophy of existence but Heidegger does not equate himself as a proponent of existentialism, rather a philosopher of Being or the being of man with its focus on ontology (philosophy of reality). For Heidegger, to exist in the world means, "We are, without our finding any reason for our being; hence, we are existence without essence"[53]

The atheistic tone in Heidegger's matches Nietzsche's rhetoric that, "God does not exist!" "We are just existents, living on earth for no apparent reason and essences are merely constructions from existences. No doubt one may seek out essences of material things and implements but there can be no essence of an existent individual, of man. Limited by death, his existence is a 'being for death."[54] Heidegger and Nietzsche present such a bleak outlook for man. If we are just beings composed of matter that evolves over time without purpose or eternal importance, the thought of this provoke a sense of despair. Heidegger concurs with this notion of despair in man's existence. Contrary to what God tell us, the Lord states

---

[53] Jean Wahl, *A Short History of Existentialism*, trans. Forrest Williams and Stanley Maron (New York: The Wisdom Libraries, 1949), 13.
[54] Ibid., 14.

through Paul in Acts 17:28-29, "...*for 'In him we live and move and have our being.'* As even some of your own poets have said, 'For we are indeed his offspring.' Being God's offspring, we ought to not think that the divine being is like gold or silver or stone, an image formed by the art and imagination of man." The message here is that we are God's creatures created in His image and as such we have worth and dignity.

Turning our attention back to Bultmann, how does he use Heidegger's philosophy of existentialism (being) in the concept of sin, salvation and church? According to Bultmann, man does not have a sinful nature nor is he considered sinful because of his sinful actions. Man's sinfulness is a total "orientation." In Bultmann's viewpoint, part of being a human is to be sinful. The sinfulness in each man identifies him as to who he is. Therefore sin is something that God condemns in a concrete present moment. Thus, when Jesus spoke of sin, He did not preach that all men are sinful. On the contrary Jesus only addressed His speeches to sinful men.

What is implied here? Man is only responsible for what he can do. Bultmann rejects the doctrine of original sin or inherited sin. The idea is in direct contradiction to what the Scriptures state in Eph. 2:1, "And you were dead in trespasses and sins in which you once walked following the course of this world...Our sins are ...ever before me" (Ps. 51:3). Jesus also warns us that "Temptations to sin are sure to comes..." (Luke 17:1).

Finally, 1 John 1:8, states, *"If we say we have no sin, we deceive ourselves, and the truth is not in us."* The rejection of the original sin is not a novel idea by Bultmann. It was introduced by a well-known Christian teacher by the name of Pelagius who taught between 383-424 A.D. in Rome. His teachings were considered heresy in May 418 A.D.

If sin is not inherited, then what is the purpose of salvation? What is it that we are saved from if there's no original sin? Salvation according Bultmann starts when "we open our hearts to the grace of God, our sins are forgiven; we are released from the past." Bultmannn's statement of salvation implies man's ability to exact his salvation, ignoring the fact that faith is a free gift of God and the submission of oneself to God's sovereign lordship. The concept of salvation is defined as an attitude of faith living "…in the unseen with that which is not at man's disposal. It gives up all of its self-created securities."[55] Bultmann describes this phase in mankind as "authentic life."

Authentic life is described as, "The life of salvation is possible in faith in God's grace, that is, in the faith that precisely the invisible, that which come to man from beyond the scope of his powers of command, means for him not death but life. This grace is forgiving grace; it frees man from the past which holds him in bondage. This faith

---

[55] Robert D. Knudsen, *Roots and Branches. The Quest For Meaning and Truth in Modern Thought,* ed. Donald Knudsen (Grand Rapids: Paideia Press, 2009), 283.

is faith in Jesus Christ through whom is made possible the obedience in love which allows one to live authentically in the present."[56]

Authentic living or "salvation" according to Bultmann is also an ever renewing process; actualized in "the event of Jesus Christ." By taking the "event of Jesus Christ" and removing it from its historical place in human history, all kinds of interpretations as perceived by society and its culture are allowed. Essentially the life of Jesus Christ would be an interpretation according to one's culture. The "event of Jesus Christ" (considered the eschatological event – end times) according to Bultmann is exemplified in the preaching and teaching of the church to an "eschatological community." Through the preaching and teaching of eschatological event, salvation will take place.[57]

Salvation as described in Rom 8:28-30 indicates that, *"We know that for those who love God all things work together for good, for those who are called according to his purpose. For those whom he foreknew he also predestined to be conformed to the image of his Son, in order that he might be the firstborn among many brothers. And those whom he predestined he also called, and those whom he called he also justified, and those whom he justified he also glorified."* Salvation is a continuous process starting with faith as a free gift of God. As is stated in Ps. 3:8, *"Salvation belongs to*

---

[56] Knudsen, Ibid *The Quest For Meaning and Truth in Modern Thought*, 284.

[57] I wonder if Bultmann is specifically referring to the "end-time remnant." In the end it does not matter for his concept is not based on Scripture.

the Lord." Acts 4:12 *"And there is salvation, for there is no other name under heaven given among men by which we must be saved."* The process of restoring one's relationship with God continues with justification (determined to be right by God), sanctification (the process of being holy in heart) and glorification, (Christ return, resurrection of the body and eternity). The fulcrum of our salvation is not in our faith but the completed work of Jesus Christ executed on the cross in history. Faith is belief in the work wrought by Jesus Christ and it continues throughout salvation.

The church's role in humanity according to Bultmann is to proclaim the Gospel as it relates to modern man and his modern understanding of things. The Gospel needs to be declared to mankind in language that is understandable, that is, a language that is cognizant of the influence of technology and science in the contemporary world. The error in Bultmann's theology is that in his desire to communicate an understanding of man's existence and a more scientific Christian faith, fundamental truths are lost. He knew that but allowed it to happen. He believed that sacrificing essential truths was alright as long as the New Testament was released from its presumed mythology.

These essential truths that were forfeited would include the doctrine of sacrificial atonement, the deity and ascension of Christ and any other truth or doctrine deemed supernatural or "mythical." Doing so, Bultmann maintained, the true meaning of Scripture would be evident. Thus the Bible no longer stood for absolute truth. On the contrary, for Bultmann, the Bible should be read subjectively in order to impart an understanding on one's existence and existential situation. This liberal interpretation of Scripture attracted the "freedom" seeking mentality of the 1960's. The other theologian, Paul Tillich had great influence in the 60's not only in theology but even in the lifestyle of the sixties decade.

Paul Tillich

"Each year at the University of Chicago Divinity School they have what is called, 'Baptist Day.' On this day each one is to bring a lunch to be eaten outdoors in a grassy picnic area. Every 'Baptist Day' the school will invite one of the greatest minds to lecture in the theological education center. One year they invited Dr. Paul Tillich. Dr. Tillich spoke for two and one half hours, proving that the resurrection of Jesus was false. He quoted scholar after scholar and book after book. He concluded that since there was no such thing as the historical resurrection, the religious tradition of the church was groundless, emotional, mumbo-jumbo, because it was based on a relationship with a risen Jesus, who, in fact, never rose from the dead in any literal sense.

After about 30 seconds, an old dark-skinned preacher with a head of short-cropped, wooly white hair stood up in the back of the auditorium. 'Docta Tillich, I got a question, he said as all eyes turned toward him. He reached into his sack lunch and pulled out an apple and began eating it. 'Docta Tillich. (CRUNCH, MUNCH) My question is a simple question. (CRUNCH, MUNCH…), Now, I ain't never read them books you read (CRUNCH, MUNCH), and I don't recite the Scriptures in the original Greek. (CRUNCH, MUNCH…) I don't know nothin' about Niebuhr and Heidegger. (CRUNCH, MUNCH…) He finished the apple. 'All I wanna know is: This apple I just ate…Was it bitter or sweet?

Dr. Tillich paused for a moment and answered in exemplary scholarly fashion: 'I cannot possibly answer that question, for I haven't tasted your apple.' The white-haired preacher dropped the core of his apple into his crumpled paper bag, looked up at Dr. Tillich and said calmly, 'Neither have you tasted my Jesus.' The 1,000 plus in attendance could not contain themselves. The auditorium erupted with applause and cheers. Dr. Tillich thanked the audience and promptly left the platform. Have you tasted Jesus? *'Taste and see that the Lord is good: blessed is the man who takes refuge in Him. If you have, rejoice in the hope of the resurrection that your faith in Him brings'* (Ps. 34:8).[58]

Tillich, who hailed from Germany, came to the U.S.A. to escape Hitler's reign of terror during WWII. While in Germany, Tillich developed the method of correlation. The technique is an effort to tie the Christian faith to all aspects of human situations and experiences. But as in incidences of finding a common ground, one runs the

[58] Personal e-mail message.

risk of compromising the faith. Tillich was a Marxist at heart and a recognized leading figure in continental theology (Christian theology based on the philosophers in Europe). He directed his energies in the definition of love, man's journey in finding love, the love of God and the interplay of both. That being said, Tillich's life search for the meaning of love included adultery, experimentation with drugs and sex, and stretching the limits of conventional morality. His writings, the greatest considered is *Systematic Theology,* was influenced by existential theology, Freudian psychology, and Marxist social theory. In Tillich's quest for the meaning of love, "…his theological endeavor was to reconsider and to reinstate the meaning of the word God."[59]

Tillich shunned conventional knowledge. He was in favor of autonomy redefined to mean freedom as a rejection of authority, resulting in a rejection of all supernaturalism and eventually idealism. Tillich's beliefs included sin as redefined to mean an estrangement from the essence of man. The Incarnation is perceived as never have taken place because God could never become man. The reason according to Tillich? For God to become man he would have to cease to be God and He cannot do that.

---

[59] Charles Henderson, "Paul Tillich: Theism Rewritten for an Age of Science" www.godweb.org/Tillich.htm

Conclusion

Sociologists and theologians view religion and the Christian faith as a function of social integration and social traditions just as the institution of marriage, births, and deaths. A shift has taken place from the traditional view of Christian faith being central in society to one reduced to a mere social symbol, an artifact of society. Jesus Christ is minimized to a figure of a past culture and only reinterpreted as a representation that reflects the present cultural values.

Indeed the Bible is <u>not</u> a collection of myths from a time and place from long ago. Nor do Scripture reflect or chronicle the story of a bygone culture. The Scriptures tell of timeless truths that will speak to people anywhere in time, space, location and culture. All can associate with the truths that were written by man and inspired by God; the inerrant words of God. Thus, the Scriptures speak a common language, a language that can be understood by all, at all times. It bridges cultures and all societal groups. So simple is its messages that it does not require any fancy methodologies or inquiry. Yet man, in his quest to out better God continues to question, doubt and even try to improve the words of God contained in the Scriptures.

The mood of society during the 60's could be best described by noted historian Arthur M Schlesinger, Jr. as "crisis in confidence." and likened it to the slavery issue during the 1850's-1860's which eventually caused a crippling civil war. Undeniably the spirit of the 1960's which whispered half-truths in the ears of society caused it to revolt against the clearly defined truths of Scripture. Past and present scenarios exemplify man's desire for godhead causing spiritual battle among man; a civil war between flesh and spirit. As foretold by Peter, *"Beloved, I urge you, as sojourners and exiles to abstain from the passions of the flesh, which wage war against your soul* (1Peter 2:11).

The next chapter discusses the 1970's. The decade was commonly called the "Me-Decade." Ten years illustrated the effort to satisfy the desires of the flesh. The synthesis that emerged between the thesis of God's Word and its antithesis of intelligent faith is tolerance. Tolerance becomes the antithesis for the 1970's. Once again clashes occurred as tolerance is pitted against the Word of God.

Chapter Five

❧ ❧❧

THE 1970'S – THE "ME-DECADE"

"**A**n old man writer says, 'Faith and Reason may be compared to two travelers: Faith is like a man in full health, who can walk his twenty or thirty miles at a time without suffering. Reason is like a little child who can only, with difficulty, accomplish three or four miles. 'Well,' says the old writer, 'on a given day Reason says to Faith, 'O good Faith, let me walk with thee.' Faith replies, 'O Reason, thou can'st never walk with me!' However, to try their paces they set out together, but they soon find it hard to keep company. When, they come to a deep river, Reason says, 'I can never ford that,' but Faith wades through singing. When they reach a lofty mountain, there is the same exclamation of despair; and in such cases, Faith, in order not to leave Reason behind, is obliged to carry him on his back; and adds the writer, 'Oh! What a luggage is Reason to Faith'"[60]

The social issues of civil rights, anti-war stances and the resistance of all forms of authority that galvanized the American public in the 1960's continued into the 1970's. The race issue of the African American started to morph into other areas after the assassination of Martin Luther King, Jr. and Senator Robert Kennedy. The civil rights advocacy evolved to include a feminist cause and movement.

So great was this movement that the 1970's decade came to be known for its "second wave feminism (The first wave started at the beginning of the 20th century.) Thus 1970's saw the dawning of feminism unlike that of 50 years prior with the assertion of humanistic values. Consequently the wave of humanistic values that gripped American society led to acceptance of abortion, moral decay, prayer ousted from public forums and the promotion of evolution.

In contrast with the sixties decade where the focus was on things external to oneself, the 1970's emphasis was on the individual. The decade was thus dubbed the "Me Decade." Humanism during this period of time continued to flourish in popularity. An updated version of the Humanist Manifesto II appeared in 1973 (The first manifesto was published in 1933).

---

[60] Henry Davenport Northup, D.D., *Life and Works of Rev. Charles H. Spurgeon* (Cincinnati: Forshee and McMakin, 1891), 463.

The society in 1973 was ripe to receive the Humanist Manifesto II. In the bestseller book of 1970, "The Greening of America," author Charles Reich writes, "There is a revolution coming. It will not be like revolutions of the past. It will originate with the individual and with culture and it will change the political structure only as its final act. It will not require violence to succeed, and it cannot be successfully resisted with violence. It is now spreading with amazing rapidity, and already our laws, institutions and social structure are changing in consequence... This is the revolution of the new generation."[61]

Armed with a declaration, (the Humanist Manifesto II) the 1970's announced it was the "dawn of a new age... Using technology wisely, we can control our environment, conquer poverty, markedly reduce disease, extend our life span, significantly modify our behavior, alter the course of human evolution and cultural development, unlock vast new powers, and provide humankind with unparalleled opportunity for achieving an abundant and meaningful life... We affirm a set of common principles that can serve as a basis for a secular society on a planetary scale."[62]

The Humanist Manifesto II sought to design and reengineer society for a "better" one that "...strives for the good life, here and now." The feminist movement also used the manifesto to navigate through any or all possible

---

[61] Charles A. Reich, *The Greening of America* (New York: Bantam Books, 1971), 2.
[62] Humanist Manifesto II www.secularhumanism.org.

objections to their agenda. The seventies was a decade extremely favorable for women. The feminists were buoyed by the inspiring words from the Humanist Manifesto II, that stated, "In the area of sensuality, we believe that intolerant attitudes often cultivated by orthodox religions and puritanical cultures, unduly repress sexual contact. The route to birth control, abortion and divorce should be recognized… neither do we wish to prohibit, by law or social sanction, sexual behaviors between consenting adults. The many varieties of sexual behavior should not in themselves be considered evil… a civilized society should be a tolerant one."

Linda Gordon, feminist, went as far as to state, "The nuclear family must be destroyed… Families have supported oppression by separating people into small, isolated units, unable to join together for common interests." Basically feminism sought to transform traditional marriage and family in order to eliminate sex roles and perceived patriarchal obstruction. The goal was essentially to achieve a woman's self-fulfillment and the realization of alternative lifestyles.[63]

Accompanying the second wave of feminism was the emergence of a militant type of environmentalism. Its first victory was celebrated on April 22, 1970; the official "Earth Day" holiday. The new holiday was to be honored in all educational institutions. Moreover, 1973 heralded a

[63] See Karl Marx, *The Communist Manifesto*, where Marx specifically urges for the "abolition of family!" In its place will be a "community of women" because marriage is considered prostitution.

landmark ruling in the Supreme Court legalizing abortion during the early months of pregnancy.

The Equal Rights Amendment to the Constitution was passed by Congress which stated that "equality of rights under the law shall not be denied or abridged by the U.S. or any state on the account of sex." (It has yet to be ratified by all 51 states.) Other fallouts as a consequence of the seventies influence include the legalization of no fault divorce which originated in California in 1970 and fully accepted by all states by October 2010. The gay movement saw its opportunity to move its agenda towards acceptance, all in the name of tolerance. Ultimately both the feminist and gay movements produced huge victories in the changing traditional conceptions.

Originally the gay movement in the 1970's was isolated in urban areas such as San Francisco and New York. The changing social climate of tolerance allows for gay culture to be openly expressed. Great strides were made politically during this decade and figures such as Harvey Milk were elected to influential government positions who advocated anti-gay discrimination laws. Similar to the feminist sentiments, the themes of the gay movement were focused on traditional family lifestyle and heterosexual chauvinism. The effort was to establish civil rights to all areas of gay lifestyle. The gays and feminists proved to be formidable forces imposing upon the church.

Equality is a universal concept that is even discussed in the Bible. But what does Scripture state about equality of the sexes? The complementarian view focuses on the theological perspective in Christianity that men and women are complementary in their relationships. The premise maintained is that men and women were designed by God to be in balance or harmonizing in relationships and in ministries (Gen. 2:18, 21-24, Cor. 11:7-9, 1Tim. 2:12-14).

The notion of male headship does not imply inferiority of women. Nor does male headship mean male dominance as Biblical headship does not seek to control or oppress. The role as helper brings a unique perspective to the definition of a woman (the term "helper" in this context is defined as someone who lends a hand or helps out, most often used in the context of God's relation to Israel).

Women's role as helper therefore does not carry with it any implication of subordination. Women have different roles and responsibilities which are reflected in marriage, family life, church, and elsewhere. When we understand God as our helper, we begin to realize the depth and power of the female design and purpose.

Some object to these distinctions as defined in the Bible because they argue that cultural situations in the ancient world were different then today. Back then, women were not well educated. Women today are educated and have many gifts to share so they should not be limited by their gender. True that women are more educated today than Biblical times and have many gifts to share but the gifts that God endowed women are to be used within the guidelines of Scripture.

Considering the events that took place in American society over the past two decades; the issues of civil rights including the feminist and gay issues, racism, the urgency of humanistic values and environmentalism would prove to be a challenge to the church. One word that would describe the call of the 70's decade would be tolerance, its antithesis. The churches as representatives of Christ would have to be the counter. What would they do?

"Mere tolerance is the virtue of man who no longer believes in anything." G.K. Chesterton

After decades of social unrest and turmoil, the mainline churches found themselves at a crossroad. It became apparent to the leaders of the churches in the 1970's that they were in an age that belonged to the people. That is, the contention that the churches' authority came from above no longer sufficed.

Instead the church leaders realized that their authority was starting to come from below, at the grassroots level. To some of the practical church leaders, they took their shoes off in a manner of speaking and went barefoot in order to feel the grass stirring beneath their feet. The church leaders who walked barefoot among the grass during the 1970's would feel the antithesis of tolerance. Churches found themselves cornered.

To insist on the Word of God would be perceived as being bigoted. Bigotry was not what the mainline churches of the 1970's wanted to be portrayed as, especially when financial support had dramatically dropped.

In 1933, Monsignor Fulton J. Sheen, a Catholic wrote in an essay entitled, "A Plea for Intolerance," that America is not suffering from intolerance. It is suffering from tolerance. Tolerance of right and wrong, truth and error, virtue and evil, Christ and chaos…Tolerance is an attitude of reasoned patience toward evil…a forbearance that restrains us from showing anger or inflicting punishment. Tolerance applies only to persons…never to truth. Tolerance applies to erring, intolerance to the error…"[64] A secular definition of tolerance may include a state or character that exhibits lenience, patience, long-suffering, allowing something to be without opposition.

Bernard Iddings Bell, (1886-1958) an Episcopal pastor who wrote more than 20 books analyzing the American paradigm for living once wrote about the current social state of affairs as, "A great upheaval of life and thinking through what humanity has gone has been accompanied, first, by a popular sense of uncertainty about everything and a consequent tolerance that during periods of strife in human history, compromise is reached and life resumes with a new meaning."[65]

---

[64] Monsignor Fulton J. Sheen, "A Plea for Intolerance"
http://www.alliance4lifemin.org/articles/php?id=158.
[65] Bernard Iddings Bell, *Unfashionable Conviction* (New York: Brothers Publication, 1931), 89.

Today if you "google" tolerance you will find many websites that instruct children and teachers how to teach tolerance. Some have school activities that "explore gender stereotypes through dance," "camps" that train student leaders to use activities that explore "identity and the understanding of themselves, "having two dads" and why it is not a problem, "subtle messages [that] shape students." The list seems endless.

In most people's perspectives and clearly in the perspective of the churches up till now to be other than tolerant would prove one to be a bigot. Well, what is so horribly wrong to be thought of as a bigot? Consensus tells us that bigot or bigotry denotes one that is unyielding, obstinate and stubborn, who is tied to a certain cause. For Bell, "Tolerance is a destructive force; the succeeding intolerance is constructive. The danger of tolerance is always this, that people may assume it to be a final instead of a preliminary step in thought adjustment, the consequence contentedly stand half-developed, intellectually immature, vitally ineffective.

The danger of tolerance is that it may destroy within us the capacity for constructive thought and determined action. "[66] Bell's argument uses Scripture to solidify his premise. He states that if Jesus wanted to demonstrate and practice tolerance, He would have not gone to the Pharisees and Sadducees during his time on earth and seek conciliation and mutual respect for their differences.

---

[66] Bell, *Unfashionable Conviction*, 90.

Instead Jesus stood firm about His Father's Word and causing so much controversy that people plotted to take his life. He did this because He came to tell the truth; to save mankind from lies and from sin!

The truth offended the Pharisees and Sadducees. Jesus was *intolerant* of their beliefs, traditions, and teachings. Matt 15:10-13 states, *"And he called the people to him and said to them, 'hear and understand; it is not what goes into the mouth that defiles a person, but what comes out of the mouth; this defiles a person.' Then the disciples came and said to him, 'Do you know the Pharisees were offended when they heard this saying.' He answered, 'Every plant that my heavenly Father has not planted will be rooted up. Let them alone; they are blind guides.'"*

There is no doubt about what Jesus stood for, the truth, God's Word. He even died for it instead of tolerating the religious ideology of that time. So great was His mission to teach His Father's Word that he implored his disciples to go out and teach mankind the Truth. *"And Jesus came and said to them, 'all authority in heaven and on earth has been given to me. Go therefore and make disciples of all nations, baptizing them in the name of my Father and the Son and the Holy Spirit, teaching them to observe all that I have commanded you. And behold, I am with you, to the end of the age"* (Matt. 28:18-20). Jesus prayed for all mankind to be united *"...united on the positive and definite platform* on which He Himself stood. Any other interpretation would stultify, not merely His words, but His whole life."[67]

Jesus stood on definite grounds, on fundamental truths that serve as a framework to our thinking that defines us who we are and how we are to relate to each other. In other words Jesus defines our "being," we identify ourselves with Him. He gave us the basis for how and what to think in order to have a clear perspective of reality, the reality that God wants us to experience. Our logic originates from here.

An Example:

"Adam and Eve's *disobedience* to God are not called sin; nowhere is there a hint that this disobedience has corrupted man. On the contrary, the disobedience is the condition for man's self-awareness, for his capacity to choose, and thus in the last analysis this first act of disobedience is man's step toward freedom." Erich Fromm[68]

During the 60's and 70's sin was redefined as a sickness in need of therapy. For example, crime was considered an antisocial behavior. A great proponent of this perspective is Erich Fromm (1900-1980), prominent psychoanalyst, social theorist, father of feminism, and critical theorist.

---

[67] Bell, *Unfashionable Conviction*, 96.
[68] Erich Fromm, *The Heart of Man* (New York: Harper and Row Publishers, 1964), 19-20.

Fromm, an atheist, defines original sin as freedom (a complete reversal of conventional logic). Man is free to commit whatever feels good to him without constraints imposed on him from authoritative entities that would determine his direction in life. Any "sinful" act, that is any human act that is deemed by society as harmful in a broad sense is considered an illness that warrants intervention using scientific methodology. As such, the crime/sin had to be treated by the psychiatrist and not by the priest or pastor of one's church.

But let's step back and take a look at sin and freedom. A secular definition of sin would include nonconformity, a deliberate action or offense against a standard. Biblically, sin is defined as "...not only the absence of good. It also entails our active opposition to God. It is then, the defiance of his authority, the rejection of his truth, the challenge to his sovereignty in which we set ourselves up in life to live the way we want to live. It is the way we wrench ourselves off from his grasp and refuse to let him be God. It is therefore all the ways we live on our terms, accountability to no one but ourselves."[69]

Sin actually predates the creation of the world with the disobedience and revolt of Lucifer (Satan) and other angels against God. In the book of Jude, verse six, it states, *"And the angels who did not stay within their own position of authority, but left their proper dwelling, he has kept in*

---

[69] David Wells, *The Courage to Be Protestant* (Grand Rapids: Eerdmans Publishing Co., 2008), 102.

eternal chains under gloomy darkness until the judgment of the great day." 2Pet. 2:4 states, "For if God did not spare angels when they sinned, but cast them into hell and committed them to chains of gloomy darkness to be kept until the judgment."

Finally, the wonderfully lofty word "freedom" is a word that man aspires to achieve and is used artfully by the enemy to deceive. Our Lord beautifully and plainly states, "Now the Lord is the Spirit where the Spirit of the Lord is, there is freedom." Although the freedom mentioned is unspecified, it is most likely the freedom that comes from salvation in Jesus and the presence of the Holy Spirit. Think of it. Through the sacrifice of Jesus and the indwelling Holy Spirit, we are free from condemnation of sin, freedom from guilt, death, free to see, feel, and hear the Gospel, as well as free access to our loving Father-God.

We have freedom to lay our burdens at the Lord's feet. This is true freedom. According to Dr. David Wells, when we rebuke God in order to go on our merry way, we tell God we are "… disaffected with your rules, resent his claim in our lives, are hostile to his truth in the biblical Word, and are determined to pursue our own values, goals, and pleasures in defiance of what he has said, This 'freedom' from all that God is, and all that he has said, turns out to be an illusion. When we freed ourselves in these way, beginning with the fall, we fell headlong into a dark captivity both to our own selves and, beyond that, to the powers of darkness."

Wells continues by stating the consequence of a false freedom, that is, freedom not from God. He states, "We imagine that within ourselves we have power enough, wisdom enough, and strength enough to live in security, in the fullness of happiness, as we want to live, amidst all the conflicts and opportunities of life. Very finite preoccupations are therefore substituted for those that are eternal, and we then confidently take the place of God once had. If the perspective of reality is changed, then the perspective of sin is changed. We therefore redefine reality."[70]

The Churches

The churches started a frantic search for relevancy in society. "At every church conference and convocation and finance committee meeting the cry was, 'We must reach the urban young people."[71] The churches started to look at issues concerning race, poverty, youth rebellion and the Vietnam war .

The year 1970 witnessed church money invested in programs such as inner city organizations and partnerships, poverty programs and novel educational ventures. The first to demonstrate relevance in society was the Lutheran Church of America. It was the largest and most liberal Lutheran denomination and the first to allow ordination of women. By 1971 the churches were embroiled in

[70] Wells, *The Courage to Be Protestant*, 102, 103.
[71] Tom Wolf, "The Me – Decade" http://www.gale.cengage.com/pdf/samples/sp656755.pdf.

controversies between denominations and church groups who advocated activist causes. A Gallop poll taken during that time demonstrated that a majority of the American population thought that Christian religion in the U.S. had entered "evil days." So contentious were the times that older clergy were considering leaving religious life while the younger clergy believed it was time to change Christianity in order to "help it."

The growing concern of "becoming;" as finding oneself resonated in the 70's decade. Where once the people of the 1960's sought to seek clarification of themselves and quench a spiritual thirst through drugs and meditation, the 1970's experienced turbulent waves of drugs, sex, ecumenism, Orientalism, Marxism, Hegelian logic and socialism. In theology there was Social gospel, the Jesus Movement, the new "religion," Scientology, the resurgence of the Church of Satan and occultism, and an attitude of "being man is no different from the divine."

Doctrinal controversies between conservatives and liberals festered especially among large denominations. To review a couple of movements of the decade, the Jesus Movement organized by the "Jesus people" was headed by Arthur Blessett, an evangelist from California. The movement ranged from youth groups organized in mainline churches to small cults with highly controversial theology. Social gospel, another movement, was not new to the scene but it was gaining momentum.

Adherents to social gospel believe that industrial capitalists, societal and economic structures set up individuals for failure, thus their sinful lifestyle. Drawing from Marxism, the Social Gospellers favored an environment for the individual with greater government involvement, labor rights and other socialist ideas such as community and its relationships to the individual. The government would be given the responsibility to enforce moral reforms.

Social Gospel proponents believed that if societal woes and adverse economic situations are eradicated then the individual would not lead a sinful lifestyle. The individual could walk away from their sinful living. This is contrary to the conventional Protestant stance that a regenerate individual will lead to social improvement. An inward transformation would have to take place, not an exterior one. As stated in Matt 11:28-30, *Jesus invites all who are burdened to come to Him. He will provide rest for those that are burdened with sin and desire to free themselves from its bondage. Eternal rest is offered to those who repent of their sins.* Consequently, as stated in Heb. 7:25, *"...he is able to save to the uttermost those who draw near to God through Him, since he always lives to make intercession for them."*

In contrast, Social Gospel adherents interpreted these verses as a "...reaction to self-centered pietism, many believed that Christians had never earnestly tried this ideal ethic of Christ and that such an effort, informed by the gospel, reinforced in worship and prayer, and empowered by the Holy Spirit could bring into being the Kingdom of God on earth. This was reinforced by faith that God was working continuously through the process of natural evolution to make men more rational and less barbarous and was transforming social structures into patterns of justice.[72]

Meanwhile the churches such as the Baptists were very concerned with secularism and its increasing effects on Christian values. The Lutherans were battling with the issue of women ordination, "doctrinal pluralism" and women's rights which included the Supreme Court decision to legalize abortion. The Presbyterians, the Reformed and the Congregational churches were focused on ecumenism while the Methodists emphasized evangelism.

Membership in the mainline churches was decreasing in the midst of increasing growth among the fundamentalism, evangelical denomination and charismatic revival. The move to achieve ecumenical agreements and understanding among various Christian denominations was growing as well as concern over the decline of Biblical absolutes. Unbelievably the strife in the mainline churches was taking place amid scientific inquiries directed on new biological and psychological techniques for controlling behavior and redesigning human nature. Eastern philosophical thought systems were

---

[72] Albert Terrill Rasmussen *Christian Social Ethics. Exerting Christian Influence* (Englewood Cliffs: Prentice – Hall, Inc., 1956), 134.

suddenly appealing as well as discussion in the proper role of government and the justice of war.

The year 1973 marked a serious reassessment of the church's role as a societal institution and its participation in the life of the individual believer. The trend toward conservatism had started as a backlash to ordination of women, denial of the infallibility of the Bible and social activism. The social, economic, and cultural factors of American society were taking its toll on Christian theology.

The mainline churches reached a crisis. The in house turmoil was evident in all denominations with threats of split. Churches were theologically pitted against each other even over splits engendering property ownership. Litigation marked 1977 when traditional separation of state and church and the not so delineated "boundaries" were challenged. Government intrusion prompted a crisis to erupt when the IRS demanded churches to submit annual informational returns from the "not integrated auxiliaries" of the churches. The National Labor Relations Board also weighed in with secular concerns for teachers in religious schools.

In other court battles parental rights versus children involved in cults were challenged. The issue of homosexuality came close on the heal of feminism but the general negative stance by the end of the 1970's towards change by the churches squashed all hope of changing church policies. The only issue that liberals and conservatives were united in the 70's was the television producers and advertisers that were promoting and showing sex and violence on primetime television.

Conclusion

The seventies decade provided opportunities grounded in its antithesis of tolerance. The pressure for churches to change or risk losing their place in society was great. Instead of standing up just as Jesus did before the Pharisees and Sadducees, they compromised. The true thesis, God's Word as delivered in the churches did not hold up. God's Word was reinterpreted as bigotry which then led to a compromise in the form of tolerance.

Tolerance was understood as social justice for gender, acceptance of what was once considered deviant behavior and counter to the specific precepts of the Lord, our God. These precepts are found in 1 Cor. 11:11, *"Nevertheless, in the Lord woman is not independent of man nor man of woman; for as woman was made from man, so man is now born of woman."* 1 Cor.9-10, 15-17 *"...Do not be deceived; neither the sexually immoral, nor idolaters, nor adulterers, no men who practice homosexuality, nor thieves, nor the greedy, nor drunkards, nor revilers, nor swindlers will inherit the kingdom of God... do you not know that your bodies are members of Christ? Shall I then take the members of Christ and make them member of a prostitute? Never! Or do you not know that he who is joined to a prostitute becomes one body with her? For it is written, 'The two shall become one flesh.' But he who is joined to the Lord becomes one spirit with him."*

In Gen. 32:1-2,4, Moses writes *"When the people saw that Moses delayed to come down from the mountain, the people gathered themselves together to Aaron and said to him,' Up make us gods who shall go before us. As for this Moses, the man who brought us up out of Egypt, we do not know what has become of him... And he received the gold from their hand and fashioned it with it a graving tool and made a golden calf. And they said, 'These are your gods, O Israel, who brought you out of Egypt."*

How quickly people forget what the Lord has done in their lives. How eager people are to fashion a life for themselves and set up idols of worship in the hopes that they can live as they deem to; without connection and remorse. When one goes into agreement with homosexuality, abortion or any belief system that is not of God, we sin against God. In Deut. 28: 15-68, God explicitly lays out the consequences of disobedience. It states, *"But if you will not obey the voice of the Lord, your God or be careful to do all his commandments and his statutes that I command you today, then all these curses shall be in the field..."*

Christians and churches must stand firm, "Confess, confess, confess," as Pastor Dietrich Bonhoeffer exclaimed. 1 Peter 4:1 states, *"Since therefore Christ suffered in the flesh, arm yourselves with the same way of thinking, for whoever has suffered in the flesh has ceased from sin."* To those who submit to others and are complacent in their Christian faith, the Lord admonishes us by stating, "Woe to those who are at ease in Zion, to those who feel secure on the Mount of Samaria and the notable men of the first of the nations, to whom the house of Israel comes."

The next chapter discusses the process of Hegelian logic as it winds itself through the 1980's. The synthesis of the 1970's (tolerance) becomes the antithesis for the 1980's. How will the mainline churches react?

Chapter Six

ൟ ൟൟ

THE EIGHTIES

RELEVANCE

Thesis: *"Do not think that I have come to abolish the Law or the Prophets. I have not come to abolish them but to fulfill them. For truly, I say to you, until heaven and earth pass away, not an iota, not a dot will pass from the Law until all is accomplished. Therefore whoever relaxes one of the least of these commandments and teaches others to do the same will be called least in the kingdom of heaven, but whoever does them and teaches them will be called great in the kingdom of heaven."* **Jesus Christ in Matt. 5:11-19.**

Antithesis: "To have any responsible chance of success, popular movement must have not only institutional outlets but also ideological space to advance their goals. Thus, democratic objectives require an attack on hierarchy and violence in every area of social life, but such objectives cannot be realized unless the various fragmenting and depoliticizing ideologies (bureaucratic rationality, privatilized individualism, cynicism, and the like) are in some way subverted...much depends therefore, upon both the intent and capacity of leftist organizations and to challenge bourgeois hegemony and, at the same time, to create a counter hegemonic presence." Carl Boggs[73]

The synthesis between secularism and the churches that emerged from the chaos in the 1960's and the struggles in the1970's was tolerance. The impetus of the churches was to be an integral part of society. Their goal was to remain <u>relevant</u> thereby have <u>relevance</u> in society. In 1980's the synthesis was translated into a new populism with an emphasis on transforming American culture. In order to make a great impact on American society, the movement avoided the dynamics of assimilation into the ideological tenets of society.

To do so, would risk its pledge to autonomy. As has been observed from the new left during the 1960's and 70's, cultural action could be generated from the grass roots of society. This singular quality served to galvanize people but its lasting effect was thought not to be long lived.[74] The new secular populism of the 1980's had to have certain qualities in order to have life transforming effect and an

---

[73] Carl Boggs, *Social Movements and Political Power* (Philadelphia: Temple University Press, 1986), 158.
[74] Boggs, *Social Movements and Political Power,* 139.

attitude change. The strategy towards the attainment of this new attitude was developed from the efforts of the left radicals of the 1960's through the 70's. The new strategy would embrace already established American institutions, norms, and values instead of trying to overturn them thus ensuring autonomy. According to proponents of such an attitude change, social change would take place through "a maturation process" in things that were already in place such as civil rights, legal and constitutional freedoms and tolerance. The place to start the process would be in the community.

The new populism would center on urban areas and its institutions. Carl Boggs described what was taking place during the 1980's as, "...the thrust of popular struggles was not only more diversified but, more significantly infused with the energy of the new social movements. The feminist, ecological, cultural- and of course democratic- components of revolt came to replace the more simple and direct efforts of the earlier period...the new populists have stressed a positive, forward-looking commitment to building alternative political, social, and economic forms.

The contemporary vision is one of a transformative populism [that] presents a self-conception that goes 'beyond' existing ideologies- whether conservative, liberal, Marxist, or anarchist-enabling them to touch broad constituencies, where anxiety to recapture the integrity of family, neighborhood, and community is widespread." [75]

The populists knew that the opposition to their thesis would be the traditional values or absolute norms and truths espoused by Christians. In direct defiance to Jesus' warning in Matt.5:11-19, the new populist movement marched forward with their agenda. By 1985, thousands of "community" organizations grew across the U.S. Their focus would be on forming political clout in order to exert their influence on American society.

Such organizations that sprung up included ACORN (Association of Community Organizations for Reform Now), CED (Campaign for Economic Democracy), the Ohio Public Interest Campaign and the Berkeley Citizens Action. Even though the new populism loathed the 2- party system of the U.S. government, it committed itself to work within the Democratic party. Feminist supported such strategy and from their perspective for any formidable social and cultural change to take place, efforts needed to include "...local mobilization, direct action, small group processes, and consciousness transformation." [76]

The overarching goal of attitude changing and consequently the social transformation via the new populism was best described by Tom Hayden (remember him as the one who championed the Port Huron Statement.) He avers that America needs to transform its

[75] Ibid., 140.
[76] Boggs, *Social Movements and Political Power,* 150.

"identity." The old identity as being the land of the free is to be replaced with an "…inner tendency to desire love, warmth, art, craft, community, knowledge…The new era will be anchored with the American sense of citizenship and democracy but with a vision to change people's consciousness to societal structure- a quiet revolution. Thus greater control of one's life."[77] One of those societal structure is the church. The church would have to change too.

The strategy to transform American society is three fold. First, change the meanings that are rooted in American character and cultural values. For example, as Boggs points out, "…community self-management signifies little more than introduction of new administrative agencies; the attack on corporate priorities takes shape as a call for public 'accountability' and 'responsibility;' 'feminism' implies the development of new affirmative action programs; and so forth."

The second approach to transform society and therefore the churches is to create sensitivity to cultural traditions within each community. According to Harvey C. Boyte, an expert in the mobilization of citizens and citizenship, if the new populist can embrace these

---

[77] Tom Hayden, *The American Future: New Visions Beyond Old Frontiers* (Boston: South End Press, 1980), 33-36.

traditional family values; he/she can fight the ideologies behind them on their own turf.[78]

An example that Boyte uses is the pro family groups in defense of traditional nuclear families as a backlash to the cry of individualism, feminism, theology of freedom, and the ills of the new left. Using Hegelian logic the struggle between the opposing viewpoints will eventually create compromise which will draw the new populism closer to their agenda.

The third approach to transform society on the whole is to create a crisis or struggle in such areas as patriarchy, racism and other components of culture and the push to supplant it. Using Hegelian logic that dictates the creation of a crisis and through the struggle between a thesis and its antithesis, a synthesis or a compromise will happen. For the ones that are aware of the struggle such as the Boytes and Boggs of society, manipulation of the outcome of the struggle (its synthesis) to one's agenda or advantage would be accomplished.

The Churches:

The 1980's desired a more moderate approach to transforming society and its institution, the church. For Jesus to be escorted out of the churches, a more undetectable method needed to be exercised. Witnesses to the 60's and 70's decade were left weary with the face to face

---

[78] Harry Boyte, *The Backyard Revolution: Understanding the New Citizen Movement* (Philadephia: Temple University Press, 1980), 24-26.

confrontations. Rethinking dictated "... a more 'realistic' agenda oriented toward the 'control', regulation and rationalization of multiple forms of domination."[79] The idea of taking over social institutions such as education, media, literature, even works of art and especially the churches was deemed of upmost importance by the promulgators of the new populist movement.

The effect of the strategy was felt in Christian theology. The conservative orthodoxy of the day was transformed to embrace what was dubbed, "liberation theology." After dismal financial struggles during the 1970's, the 80's proved to fare better as the country embraced "Reagonomics" and lifting the country out of a recession. Capitalism was in full swing again in the U.S. In Christian theology, instead of promoting and supporting man's spiritual needs, Liberation theology (LT) focused on the betterment of man's physical needs.

LT started in Latin America where it addressed the plight of the poor. It spread to Europe and to North America and throughout the world. The neo-Marxist philosophy that forms the core of LT pits the poor in a dismal perspective. Scripture is used as a confirmation of their struggles and the call to free themselves from any and all oppression (social, economic, political, racial, sexual, and religious) against them. Later it was incorporated into various theologies such as black liberation theology, feminist theology, and queer theology. LT is also

---

[79] Boyte, *The Backyard Revolution: Understanding the New Citizen Movement,* 166.

responsible for the spawning of environmentalism; that is liberation of the planet earth. The idea is that the earth is assaulted by human activity that exploits its resources. Therefore, "Mother Earth" needs to be liberated from these practices.

Scriptures that were used to underpin its perspective are found in Isaiah 61:1-2. It states, *"The Spirit of the Lord God is upon me, because the Lord has anointed me to bring good news to the poor: he has sent me to bind up the brokenhearted."* Not wishing to add to current theology, LT seeks to assert itself as a new hermeneutics of the Christian faith. The experience of community is now the new hermeneutical criteria and what directs the understanding and interpretation of the Bible. The new concepts perceived in Scripture are people and community and their experience and history.

History is a pivotal aspect to LT and its interpretation of Scripture. The events of history, that is, thesis and antithesis producing a synthesis which in turn is confronted with an antithesis and a new synthesis is created has now supplanted the Godly doctrine of salvation. Salvation is man through history as an unfolding of himself where he expresses and attains his being. Hegelian logic therefore, is the real bearer of salvation.

Therefore how is LT characterized?

1). In the community, "At the social and political level, liberation is an expression of aspirations of the oppressed and people…"

2). At the historical level, "…people develop consciously their own destiny through social changes."

3). "At the religious, salvific level the liberation means liberation from sin, the ultimate source of all deviation from fraternity, of all injustice and oppression. It brings man back into communion with God and fellow man… For the first time sin was formulated in social terms as a concrete social act and not in traditional way as an abstract, and even an allegoric personification in the person of Satan, or at least, a personal act. For the first time the religious, salvific plan was explicitly linked to the human experience in a society."[80]

Conclusion

With Scripture being used to support secular ideology, the line between Christianity and secularism is blurred. Consequently, the content the churches are preaching was becoming further away from Biblical truth. For example, in the quest to find who we are as human beings, the answer lies in Matt. 5:3-11, known as the Beatitudes.

---

[80] Marion Hillar, Liberation Theology: *Religious Response to Social Problems. A Survey* (Houston: American Humanist Association, 1993), 35.

In the Beatitudes, Jesus' overall message is to love one another as he loved us. He states, *"Blessed are the poor in spirit, for theirs is the kingdom of heaven. Blessed are those who mourn, for they shall be comforted. Blessed are the meek, for they shall inherit the earth. Blessed are those who hunger and thirst for the righteousness, for they shall be satisfied. Blessed are the merciful, for they shall receive mercy. Blessed are the pure in heart, for they shall be called sons of God. Blessed are those who are persecuted for righteousness, for theirs is the kingdom of heaven. Blessed are you when others revile you and persecute you and utter all kinds of evil against you falsely on my account."*

Jesus informs us that to be blessed, that is, to be happy, one must exemplify the following qualities in his/her character. One needs to embody all the qualities as stated by Jesus such as meekness, merciful, pure in heart, etc.; not just one, not two, but all. These qualities cannot be obtained through our own merits or our innate nature but through the grace of God and the work of the Holy Spirit in us.

This important point is what separates us from the non-Christian. The non-Christian and even some professing Christians deny the grace of God and the effects of the Holy Spirit instead relying on their own capabilities. For them, these qualities are not spiritual in nature but are practical. If they are not functional then they are deemed ideological and unrealistic. Such is the case with LT. If the qualities as described in the Beatitudes cannot be worked out here and now, then the Kingdom of heaven (God) cannot be established here on earth. For them, fighting for injustice and "liberation" (from any perceivable domination) will establish the Kingdom of God on earth.

Of note the poor in spirit spoken of in the Beatitiudes are not those that are oppressed by domineering entities that create poverty. (Luke 6:20 is used by LT to substantiate the claim to poverty). Those that are "poor in spirit" are the ones that realize he/she has limits and cannot do anything before the eyes of the Lord without the help of Jesus. All one's wealth, influence, and confidence will not save him from a terrible life and death. Submissiveness, humbleness, and dependence on Jesus for salvation is the only way.

The Beatitudes begin with "Blessed are the poor in spirit, for theirs is the kingdom of heaven. Poor in spirit is the most important quality (and the reason why it is mentioned first). It sets the stage and the logical spiritual progression towards attaining entrance into the Kingdom of God (heaven). The verse is a perfect description of the doctrine of justification by faith. Realizing that there is nothing we can do to justify ourselves before God, through faith, we ask for forgiveness. Through grace, our Lord forgives us.

To clarify the Kingdom of God, let's discuss how it is established. First, the Kingdom of God is established through our Savior, Jesus Christ. Col. 1:13 states, *"He has delivered us from the domain of darkness and transferred us to the kingdom of his beloved Son."* (The Kingdom of the Son is the same as the Kingdom of God or heaven.) In Matt. 3:2, John the Baptist proclaims, *"Repent, for the Kingdom of heaven is at hand"* meaning that Jesus himself is the Kingdom of God to deliver the Good News. The second way that the kingdom of God is established is when one embarks on the path towards salvation. Paul states in his letter to the Philippians that when we believe, *"our citizenship is in heaven"* (Phil. 3:20) we are no longer in this world, although we live in it; it is only temporary. Your citizenship in heaven emphasizes the unity we share in the Kingdom of God as believers. People in this kingdom are thus considered a community. The community does not denote a geographic location or a political entity but a body of believers who have committed themselves to live under the authority of God. Through this community, the church is created.

The community of believers, "constitute a Kingdom in their relationship to God in Christ as their ruler, and a Church in their separateness from the world in devotion to God, and their organic union with one another."[81] Lastly, the kingdom of God will return when Christ returns at the end of time (See the book of Revelations).

The resounding argument of the 80's was what role does religion and faith have in a person's life (its relevance). Statistics revealed that by the 1980's there was a decrease in

---

[81] Louis Berkhof, *Systematic Theology* (Grand Rapids: Eerdsmans Publishers, 1938), 569.

the mainline Protestant church membership. Conversely there was a tremendous rise of religious conservatism. The conflict between conservative and liberal factions regarding the role of churches and the changes in societal norms and values caused conservatism to grow evangelical branches. The most prominent being the Pentecostals or the Assembly of God. Not considered a dominant sect during this time or Protestant, the sect did share conservative and fundamentalist views of the Bible.

The 1980's marked 3 in 10 Americans who identified themselves as an evangelical. The Evangelical movement started in the 1730's in England. It strove to maintain the inerrancy of the Bible. The movement actively expressed the Gospel while maintaining absolute truths or fundamental doctrines of Scripture. But by the 1980's, feeling the infringement of secular ideology into their faith, mobilization of Christian conservative groups emerged such as the Moral Majority led by Rev. Jerry Falwell. The groups' focus was centered towards promotion of Americans into the political arena and directed on issues affecting traditional family values, rescinding abortion laws and ministering to the unbelievers. A new Christian right was born.

The struggle to push churches to support a Christless faith marched on through the 1980's. Its effect could be measured by the weak opposition by the churches. Thus far, churches reacted with a knee – jerk attempt to counter. Scripture as the inerrant Word of God may have been consulted but it was compromised in the name of appeasement in order to remain relevant. The church which is to be the backbone to Christianity and the upholder of Truth was suffering from weakness. You could say that the backbone of the church was suffering from "severe scoliosis."

The 1990's is discussed in the ensuing chapter. The antithesis of relevance embodied in the new populism and its thesis, God's Word as reflected in the churches, produced a synthesis comprising a "new" reformation. Unlike the reformation of the 16th century, this new reformation will prove to be militant in its fervor and unbiblical in nature.

Chapter Seven

ക•ക•ക

THE 1990'S

THE NEW REFORMATION

November 4-7, 1993 marked a conference held by the World Council of Churches at the Minneapolis Convention Center. 2,200 participants attended from 27 countries and 49 states. The conference was underwritten by the Greater Minneapolis-St Paul area, the Minnesota Council of Churches, the Presbyterian Church (USA), The National Ministries of America, Baptist Church, the Board of Homeland Ministries of the United Church of Christ, the Division of Congregational Ministers, the Evangelical Lutheran Church of America, the Women's Division of the United Methodist Church and various orders of Roman Catholic nuns. The conference, entitled, "Solidarity with Women" was for women and men alike. The purpose, according to Virginia R. Mollenkolt, a femininst theologian was for "...reimagining all that has been passed to us through the 2000 years of Christian faith…to a second reformation that … is much more basic and important to the health of mankind."

Mary Ann Lundy and Bishop Forrest Steth, Presbyterian and Methodist respectively and also co-chairmen of the U.S. Committee of the Ecumenical Decade described the purpose of the conference this way. "'The need is for radical theological surgery. Our churches …must free themselves from the grip of sexism, racism, and classism.' Speaker after speaker elaborated on this theme: the Church remains 'womanless' because current doctrine and practice stifle women's voices.

Women require a new theology grounded in their unique female, everyday experience of the divine. Rather than pursuing the truth, this RE-imaging's focus was to encourage women to imagine 'her own truth.' The new reformation's aim in the words of liturgy director Sue Seed-Martin, is to create that wonderful space where we're truly free to be ourselves."[82] The RE-imaging conference offered many forms for participants to pursue "her own truth." From Native Americans, "talking circles" and "scribble writing," along with blessed "rainsticks" and "holy manna" dance were presented as avenues to pursue truth. Participants were urged to anoint themselves with red dots on the forehead to denote the "divine in each other and to

---

[82] Kathy Kerden, "A New Heaven and a New Earth" *First Things*, March, 1994 www.FirstThings.com.

protest the perceived oppression wrought by Christian missionaries." [83]

The activities and seminars of the conference forces one to question if the conference was truly Christian? What Scripture were they using to support their claims? Incredibly verses in the Bible to undergird the various proclamations in the conference were found. In Prov. 3:16; 8:30 it states, *"Long life is in her right hand; in her left hand are riches and honor" and "Then I was beside him, like a master workman, and I was daily his delight, rejoicing before him always."* Actually these two verses are used to personify wisdom, as female figure. One is urged to seek wisdom as a virtue that is desirable in a person. But sadly the female personification was transformed into a god to be worshipped by the feminists.

The perception of oppression and persecution is buoyed by a verse found in Luke 11:49 which states, *"Therefore also the Wisdom of God said, 'I will send them prophets and apostles, some of whom they will kill and persecute."* But let's put things in perspective. As a rule of thumb, in Bible hermeneutics, to confirm the true message of a verse, another verse is used to validate its veracity. It seemed that this was no longer the case. Declarations were made, using Scripture to substantiate them without researching the true meaning of the verse used. For example in both letters to the Corinthians, Paul makes clear distinctions between personal wisdom and the wisdom of

---

[83] Ibid.

God. The wisdom of God is revealed through the message of the Cross and wisdom is gained by the individual through the Holy Spirit. "Wisdom" to the organizer and participants of the conference was not from the persons of the Trinity but a pagan Greek god the conference desired. "She does not judge, nor does she recognize any sin but the corporate transgressions of racism, sexism, and classism. Sophia has only one commandment, as each participant learned – 'Freely bless your own experience.'"[84]

An altar to Sophia was erected at the Sunday service of the conference. She was to be worshipped and praised. Milk and honey was substituted for communion. The traditional way of doing communion, the way Jesus taught us in Scripture was considered a theory. As noted by a conference organizer, "I don't think we need folks hanging on crosses and blood dripping and weird stuff…We just need to listen to the god within." In a brazen move, the Lord's Prayer was summarily replaced with the following:

"Our maker Sophia, we are women in your image…With the hot blood of our wombs we give form to new life…Sophia, creator god, let your milk and honey flow…With nectar between our thighs we invite a lover, we birth a child; with our warm body fluids we remind the world of its pleasures and sensations… We celebrate the sweat that pours from us during our labors. We celebrate the fingertips vibrating upon the skin of a lover. We

---

[84] Kathy Kerden, "A New Heaven and a New Earth" *First Things*, March, 1994 www.FirstThings.com.

celebrate the tongue which licks a wound, or wets our lips. We celebrate our bodiliness, our physicality, the sensations of pleasure, our oneness with earth and water."[85] The Sunday service was brought to a close with calling all lesbians, transsexuals, bisexual women to join hands and form a circle to celebrate the "miracle of being lesbian, Christian and out!"[86]

The 90's decade was truly the decade for the advancement of the lesbian agenda so much so that 1992 was dubbed the "year of the woman." The themes of the 80's continued into the 1990's with feminism being at the top. "Girl Power" was the motto for the decade. During this period, four women were elected as U.S. senators. Globally, a record number of women served as top CEOs.

Fueled by the third wave of feminism, women and girls from all ethnicities, nationalities, cultures and experiences were encouraged to assert themselves as powerful and self-controlled individuals. They celebrated all forms of sexual expressions, even challenging mainstream beliefs toward pornography and prostitution. By 1990 the World Health Organization (WHO) removed homosexuality from its list of diseases. Homosexuality was gaining acceptance. The murder of a gay man in Wyoming ignited national anger which bolstered the lesbian, gay, bisexual, transsexual (LGBT) rights movement and its determination to eradicate homophobia. Thus the feminist

[85] Ibid.
[86] Ibid.

as well as the homosexual agendas fueled the antithesis for the 1990's.

The women and homosexual movements of the 1990's propelled the churches towards a "new reformation." During the first reformation in the 16th century, Martin Luther questioned the practices of the sole Christian church at that time, the Roman Catholic Church. "The Reformation of the 16th century made the gospel, not the ecclesiastical organization the test of the true church…the Reformation introduced *the notae ecclesia,* the marks of the church: the right preaching of God's Word and the right administration of the ordinances.

Beginning with the Reformation, then, Protestants have believed that an individual, local congregation should be regarded as the true church when the Word of God is rightly preached and the ordinances of Christ are rightly followed…The ministry of the Word, therefore is central and defining. The way to distinguish between the true church and a false church is to ask whether the church's public worship consists of right preaching of God's Word and right administration of ordinances. If both are present, a true church has formed."[87] The new reformation's aim was to revolutionize core Christian principles such as sin. As for women's rights, to excuse pre-marital sex, (into non-committal sex), pornography (into an individual right to freedom), and abortion (into a woman's right), was

---

[87] Mark Dever, *The Church. The Gospel Made Visible* (Nashville: B & H Publishing Group, 2012), 95.

denigrating the Word of God. These are all examples of declassifying sin and rebuking the Word of God.

True to the new populist movement of the 80's, social attitude change had reached the community affairs at the political and economic levels. How did the antithesis of a new reformation fare against the churches, the bearer of God's Word?

The Churches

Clearly the forces the churches had to combat during the 1990's were the drives to make homosexuality and its other branches of transsexuality, bisexual, and transvestites as normal. The violence against all forms of sexual behaviors outside of heterosexuality led to the labeling of them as minorities. As such, they were entitled to every human right and freedom. They had to be free to express their sexual preference just like any minority who wished to celebrate their ethnicity. The change from homosexuality as a moral or spiritual issue to one that was political was perceived as an issue of freedom.

The new reformation was squarely opposed to God's word as stated in 1 Cor. 6:9 where it states, *"Or do you know that the unrighteous will not inherit the kingdom of God? Do not be deceived: neither sexually immoral, nor idolaters, nor adulterers, nor men who practice homosexuality, nor thieves, nor the greedy, nor drunkards, nor revelers, nor swindlers will inherit the kingdom of God."* Rom. 1:26-27 states, *"For this reason, God gave them up to dishonorable passions. For their women exchanged relations that are contrary to nature, and the men likewise gave up relations with women and were consumed with passion with one another, men committing shameless acts with men and recurring in themselves the due penalty for their error."*

The passages address gay acts in both men and women as contrary to God's creation of them (their nature) and their powerful destructive power of this sin causing one to sin. Unrepentance for such acts as stated in Genesis, chapter one and two will be punished. So grievous is this sexual sin, that the Lord provides a way for redemption. In 1 Cor. 6:11, the Lord speaks through the apostle Paul by stating, *"But you were washed, you were sanctified, you were justified in the name of the Lord, Jesus Christ and by the Spirit of our God."* God is stating that although you have gravely sinned, you are redeemable! You can be saved. You can be washed of your sin, broken free from its influence on you. You can live a new life that is according to God's will. Truly this is an example of God's magnificent love for us.

The churches' dual responsibility is to proclaim this truth, to offer sinners hope. Through the right preaching of God's Word and the right administration of its ordinances, salvation is to be had. The second phase of responsibility is to state to a sinful society that if it continues to defy God's Word and sin, then there is no entrance into the kingdom of God.

Unfortunately Scripture is deemed out of date and in the need to bring it to the level of current culture. As for the women's agenda, unbeknownst to them, the Bible does not oppress women in a paternalistic paradigm. On the contrary, Scripture uplifts womanhood in its promotion of "dignity, honor and freedom." The well-known Baptist pastor John MacArthur explains, "Scripture never discounts the female intellect, downplays the talents and abilities of women, or discourages the right use of women's spiritual gifts. But whenever the Bible expressly talks about the marks of excellent women, the stress is always on feminine *virtue*. The most significant women in Scripture were influential not because of their careers, but because of their *character*. The message these women collectively gave is not 'gender equality'; it's about true feminine excellence. And that is always exemplified in moral and spiritual qualities rather than by social standing, wealth, or physical appearance." [88]

Pastor MacArthur continues, "Christianity, born at the intersection of East and West, elevated the status of women to an unprecedented height. Jesus' disciples included several women (Luke 8:1-3), a practice almost unheard of among the rabbis of His day. Not only that, He *encouraged* their discipleship by portraying-it's as something more needful than domestic service (Luke 10: 38-42). In fact, Christ's first recorded explicit disclosure of His own identity as the true Messiah was made by a

---

[88] John MacArthur, "The Biblical Portrait of Women: Setting the Record Straight" www.gty.org.

Samaritan woman with the upmost dignity- women who might otherwise be regarded as outcasts (Matt. 9 20-22; Luke 7:37-50; John 4:7-27). He blessed their children (Luke 18:15-16), raised their dead (Luke 7:12-15), forgave their sins (Luke 7:44-48), and restored virtue and honor (Luke 8:4-11)."[89]

Contrast this to the pagan goddess worship during the same time Jesus walked the earth, men and women continue to rebel against the Lord in the worship of idols or other gods. Pastor MacArthur puts this in its proper perspective by stating, "Pagan *religion* tended to fuel and encourage the devaluation of women…Of course, Greek and Roman mythology had its goddesses (such as Diana and Aphrodite).

But don't imagine for a moment that goddess-worship in any way raised that status of women in society. The opposite was true. Most temples devoted to goddesses were served by sacred prostitutes-priestesses who sold themselves for money, supposing they were performing a religious sacrament. Both the mythology and practice of pagan religion have usually been overtly demeaning to women. Male pagan deities were capricious and sometimes wantonly misogynistic. Religious ceremonies were often blatantly obscene-including such things as erratic fertility rites, drunken temple orgies, perverted homosexual practices, and in the very worst cases, even human

---

[89] Ibid.

sacrifices."[90] We still practice the "worst cases" today. Our human sacrifices are in the form of abortion.

A two - fold approach by the churches to stay relevant was materializing during the 1990's. The first strategy was to change the churches' mission and bylaws to include feminine and gay theology. The second strategy was to reinterpret Scripture to reflect the current times. The move prompted the Baptists to become embroiled in a ten year debate between themselves and moderates over the inerrancy all Scripture.   Whereas, the other mainline churches found "new reformation" in their respective denominations. For the Evangelical Lutherans, 1990 eased in the antithesis of reformation by suspending two San Francisco churches for five years for ordaining pastors of a lesbian couple and a homosexual man. The reason cited was not because of sexual preference but the ordination required a pledge of celibacy. By 1994 the 3.2 million members of the Evangelical Lutherans drafted a statement that included wording to promote a more liberal stance on masturbation, homosexual couples and the use of condoms to prevent diseases.

The Presbyterian Church (USA) in 1991 was faced with a recommendation from a committee during the General Assembly to abandon the church's stance on its disapproval of premarital and homosexual acts. It was rejected. The United Methodists, on the other hand, were

---

[90] MacArthur, "The Biblical Portrait of Women: Setting the Record Straight" www.gty.org.

confronted by a majority who favored striking from church laws, a statement that declares homosexual practice as "incompatible with Christian teaching." By 1992, the Methodist refused to eliminate the statement that calls homosexuality as ""incompatible with Christian teaching" but did support civil rights for all homosexuals. During that time, the United Methodists approved a new worship book. Outstanding in the new worship book was the portrayal of God as female with a strong alluding to calling the deity "Mother God."

The Episcopalians focused on forbidding pre-marital sex and the ordination of anyone who had pre-marital sex and homosexual unions. By the 1995, the trial of Walter C. Righte of Iowa was charged with heresy for ordaining a noncelibate homosexual man. Righte was outspoken for the dissent of gays in the Episcoplian Church. As former assistant bishop in Newark, New Jersey, he was under the direction of Bishop John Spong. Spong was an ardent supporter for the ordination of homosexuals and lesbians. The charges were later dropped in a 7-1 vote. The eight bishops who voted ruled that church doctrine did not forbid ordination of homosexuals and lesbians who were committed to each other. Shortly thereafter an apology was issued by the Episcopalian church for the prejudices expressed in the church against homosexuals and lesbians. Subsequently the option to extend health insurance benefits to same sex couples was offered and the ordination of women was also deemed mandatory.

As changes in church policies were being made, splits within the denominations were also occurring as a backlash to change. For example, the second female bishop for the Episcopalians caused a faction to form called the Episcopal Synod of America, later renamed the Missionary Diocese of America (MDA). Its premise was to maintain traditional parishes and clergy. For the fundamental Baptists, the Alliance of Baptists, a group of moderates separated to form an independent organization.

The mainline churches continued to experience drops in membership. So much so that many had to cut staff and programs. But surveys indicted that people were returning to church, just not to the mainline churches. They were going to Pentecostal churches that experienced massive conference attendance during the 1990's. So great was this impact that during the 1990's, the decade was dubbed, "Decade of World Evangelism." One conference in Indianapolis saw 25,000 people. On October 4, 1997, 1.5 million men convened on the Mall in Washington, D.C. They were called "the Promise Keepers." It was to be the largest religious gathering in American history. In worldwide events, Bern, Switzerland witnessed 4,000 people in attendance, 2,000 from Eastern Europe including both Protestants and Catholics.

A conference in Jerusalem attracted representatives from thirty countries. Huge revivals were held in Argentina and Central America claiming over one million conversions in one week. The motto in these conferences across the globe was "reconciliation across denomination and racial boundaries, practice spiritual moral, ethical and sexual purity and male leadership in family." The National Organization of Women (NOW) called it the greatest danger to women's rights.

At home and across the world a Baptist pastor named Pat Robertson became a formidable force during the 1990's especially in politics. Pastor Robertson could very well have represented the opposition to the new reformation. What the mainline churches lacked in proclaiming God's Word, that is the truth to the masses, Pastor Robertson and others such as Jerry Falwell and John MacArthur made up for it. Pastor Robertson's organization, The Christian Coalition made its goal to return conservative Christianity to its focal point in families. Communication media such as television and radio greatly helped the effort.

Pastor MacArthur succinctly stated on his radio show, "Grace to You" on September 2, 1992, the consequences of the mainline churches if they condone homosexual practices. He explains, "…when you declassify it as a sin, you cut them [the people] off from their salvation source… This is not an alternative lifestyle. This is not a genetic thing. This is sin and perversion that damns men's and women's souls."

Although great strides towards loosening the bonds of liberalism were made, the antithesis of new reformation against the thesis, God' Word seemed unscathed. By 1990, the new Revised Standard Version Translation of the Bible was released. The purpose of the publication according to its publishers was to affect the English language's innate bias that favors the male gender.

A conference held in Northfield, Minnesota, called "Reclaiming the Bible for Church" in 1994 attracted many theologians who alleged that certain groups such as the "Jesus Seminars" were teaching heresy. The Jesus Seminars hosted workshops and lectures throughout the U.S. and published five controversial books. They are "The Five Gospels: The Search for Authentic Words of Jesus" by Robert W. Funk, "Jesus: A Revolutionary Biography" by John Dominick Crossan, "The Lost Gospel" by Bruce L. Mack, "Meeting Jesus Again for the First Time" by Marc J. Borg, "The Religion of Jesus the Jew" by Geza Vermes and "The Book of Q" by Jonathan Rabb. The letter q in the title of the latter book is short for the German word, quelle, which means source. A document is purportedly to exist that was written before the gospel writings of Matthew and Luke.

The contention is that a small group of countercultural early believers of Jesus existed. These early followers did not believe Jesus as a messiah, prophet or that He even resurrected from death. He was simply a wise and articulate teacher who challenged the establishment of the day. The "Book of Q" records only the "wise" sayings of Jesus. One of the other books questions the number of actual gospels. There are those that state a fifth gospel exists; the gospel of Thomas. These documents considered non-canonical, came from early Christian sects that were probably Gnostic in beliefs. They were probably Gnostic because some parts are incompatible with the canonical Gospel.

Other assertions by the Jesus Seminar is the denial of apocalyptic eschatology in favor of a sapiential eschatology (a view that maintains Jesus' ministry, His words and deeds are of greater value than His messianic purpose). Proponents of this view believe Jesus came to bring a message of love and to right the wrongs of social injustice. Thus one's mission in life is to set out into the world and seek reparation. Proponents of such thinking do not believe in the inerrant word of God in Scripture. On the contrary, the gospels are considered rift with errors. They believe that there was no immaculate conception, Jesus had a human father and there were no miracles. Opinions held are that Jesus was not killed because He declared himself the Messiah but because He was a public nuisance. And there was never a resurrection that took place because it was based on the illusion of Mary Magdalene, Peter, and Paul.

Conclusion

Rom. 3:23 *"for all have sinned and fall short of the glory of God."*

Ps. 53:3 *"They have all fallen away; together they have become corrupt; there is none who does good, not even one.*

Isa.53: 6 *"All we like sheep have gone astray, we have turned-gone to his own way; and the Lord has laid on him the iniquity of us all."*

John 1:8 *" If we say we have so sin, we deceive ourselves, and the truth is not in us."*

The old adage that states that history repeats itself holds very true at this point in Christian theology. The present situation in the mainline churches was also experienced in its early history. The fifth century was marked with theological controversy. A monk from Great Britian denied original sin as well as Christian grace.

As stated in previous chapters, Pelagius, a monk, was influenced by pagan Greek philosophy. He maintained that faith rested on man's moral strength and will. According to Pelagius, faith could be augmented if asceticism is sought. He states, "This in itself is sufficient to desire and attain the loftiest ideal of virtue. Yes, one can, through a perfect life without any assistance from divine grace…The value of Christ's redemption was, in his opinion, limited mainly to instruction (doctrine) and example (exemplum) which the Savior through the balance as a counter weight against Adam's wicked example, so that nature retains the ability to conquer sin and to gain eternal life even without the aid of grace.

By justification we are indeed cleansed of our person sins through faith alone, but this pardon (gratis missionis) implies no interior renovation or sanctification of the soul."[91]   Six hundred years after the birth of Christ, the Words of God as expressed in Scripture bore little meaning to Pelagius.   Nineteen hundred years later, the same premises continue to echo.

Dr. R. C. Sproul, a contemporary Reform theologian stated, man continues to believe in"…that little island of righteousness where man still has the ability in of himself, to turn, to change, to incline, to dispose, to embrace."[92] The synthesis of the 1990's would fool man to believe in this "little island of righteousness, this "oasis" where man believes he can live a life without God's conviction. The synthesis between thesis, God's Word as expressed through the churches and its antithesis, the new reformation is deconstruction.

Deconstruction   is   a   concept   enthusiastically employed to demonstrate the alleged incoherence of an established   stance.   Hence,   deconstruction   is   highly executed on any absolute, universal or stable meaning. Its aim is to show that by placing positions, stances, doctrines, concepts into new contexts, new meanings are produced. These meanings are both different but also similar to its previous   connotation.   Placed   in   a   social   context, deconstruction   forces   one   to   acknowledge   others   from themselves, to be open to them and their perspectives. Eventually the process causes one to doubt their own beliefs as   he/she   strives   to   comprehend   the   situations   and

---

[91] The Catholic Encyclopedia Vol. XI. Charles G. Herbermann, et. al. (new York: Robert Appleton Co., 1911), 604.
[92] R. C. Sproul, *The Pelagian Captivity of the Church*" www.bible-researcher/sproul.html.

perspectives of others. Consequently deconstruction became the antithesis for the beginning of the 21st century. Feminists and proponents of liberal social justice used deconstruction extensively to redesign the female identity, sexuality, and other social constructs.

As the roots of Hegelian logic take hold in society, its growth becomes more vigorous. Bold measures, actions, and declarations as were noted, were made to preserve the "freedom" one perceives. The concept of deconstruction is considered a bold but powerful weapon to finalize the transformation of churches to a Christless faith. The next chapter will discuss the use of deconstruction in the first ten years of the 21st century.

Chapter Eight

ঔঔঔ

2000 – 2010

DECONSTRUCTION

"I actually think you can become a Christian and never even know who Jesus is… Many of my friends are now out in Muslim countries ministering. In the past we would have said we want people to convert to Christianity. We don't do that anymore. We invite people to follow Jesus. They are not even asking them to leave their Muslim faith, they are asking them to simply follow Jesus." Spencer Burke[93]

Major life changing events marked the first decade of the 21st century. An attack on the World Trade Center in New York and the Pentagon in Washington, D.C. by Muslim extremists on September, 11, 2001 forced people to

---

[93] Charlie Ware, "An Interview with Spencer Burke: Author of *A Heretics Guide to Eternity* Next – Wave August, 2006 http://www.the-next-wave-ezine.info/issue92/index.cfm?id=158ref=coverstory.

pause and ask what was happening. Suddenly there was evilness in our midst that sought to destroy us as a nation for what we represented.

A war on terror was subsequently declared with battlegrounds in Iraq and Afghanistan. As if that was not enough, Hurricane Katrina hit the southeast coast of the U.S. in 2005, decimating New Orleans. Financial problems both at home and abroad followed by the late 2000's. In other parts of the globe, Iran was anxiously pursuing nuclear armament while North Korea successfully performed nuclear test in 2006 and 2009. As if the American public suffered from Post Traumatic Stress Disorder, the pause and questioning throughout these crisis' resulted in an attitude change or an attitude adjustment. The attitude change found its basis in the antithesis of deconstruction. What was held as true was doubted. Amazingly, rapid spread was due to the worldwide use of the internet. The internet served to unite the world in the attitude change grounded in postmodern thinking employing Hegelian logic.

As a result, deconstruction as a product of postmodernism, had a stranglehold around the neck of the fledgling 21st century. Attitude change shifted to include the way one understands reality. Specifically, absolute truths no longer were the standard one used to measure anything. Where in the past an individual's intellectual capabilities (knowledge) were held in high regard, knowledge is now created by social determiners.

Cultures and subcultures in a society create their truth therefore universal truths or absolute truth no longer existed. Everything is relative. Everyone's truth is equal and deserves respect. Therefore truths that are spoken about in Scripture are perceived only as power seeking or as authoritarian. One has to ask if rights and wrongs are shunned, then where does morality or ethics stand? What guides our behavior? The only "rule" in the new attitude of the postmodern era is not to impose one's beliefs on another. To do so would be considered a cardinal sin; the the only sin recognized. Since there are no truth claims, what remains are our individual stories or narratives.

Other people have their own story and they are equally valid as our own and these determine the concepts of morals and values that become part or "our story." As a result the Bible is ousted not only as God's Word but as the source of morality, ethics or judgments. "When you let go of the Bible as God's answer book, we get it back as something much better... It becomes the family story, the story of people who have been called by the one true God to be his agents in the world, to be his servants." [94] "It is also essential to give the family a sense of identity, so we know who we are and why we're here and where we're going and not only what it's wonderfully honest about our weakness and mistakes...There's no mistaking who the hero is in this story- it's certainly not any of us humans! So...we need to

---

[94] Brian McLaren, *A New Kind of Christianity* (San Francisco: Jossey-Bass, 2001), 74. In this fictional book, McLaren uses the protagonist, Neo as the mouthpiece to expresses his Christian beliefs.

let it go as a modern answer book, we get to rediscover it for what it really is: an ancient book of incredible value for us, a kind of universal and cosmic history book that tells us who we are and what story we find ourselves in it that we know what to do and how to live."[95]

The Bible is now a history book where people find out who they are. Really? The true purpose of the Bible has been deconstructed to mean whatever one wants it to means. If ever there was a contradiction, it is illuminated in 2 Tim. 3:16, which states, *"All Scripture is breathed out by God and profitable for teaching, for reproof, for correction, and for training in righteousness, that the man of God may be competent, equipped for every good work."* Paul specifically states in the verse that all scripture is divine and thus authoritative, the final word. Scripture has the power to transform people and to be used in a variety of ways that would lead one to righteousness. Instead, deconstruction has denied the power of the Word and relegated it to some dusty relic of the past.

At the start of the 21st century, a new antithesis, deconstruction, served as a tool to tear down all meanings. Words were gutted and reworked to one's liking. Not only did deconstruction march forward with a machete cutting down meanings and words used in everyday life, it also did a hatchet job in Christian theology. There was nothing untouched in Christian theology.

---

[95] McLaren, *A New Kind of Christianity*, 75.

"I warn everyone who hears the words of the prophesy of this book: if anyone adds to them, God will add to him plagues described in this book, and if anyone takes away from the words of this prophesy, God will take away his share in the tree of life and in the holy city which is described in this book." Jesus in the book of Revelation 22: 18-19.

If meaning is derived from the social or cultural construct then how does this remedy itself in Christian theology? Traditional Christian theology maintains a certain amount of foundational doctrines or absolutes that form the basis of our faith. Rejecting all forms of objective truth, a search for spirituality is sought instead. According to D.A. Carson, "This works out in an emphasis on feelings and affection over linear thought and rationality: on experience over against truth; on inclusion over against exclusion; on participation over against individualism and the heroic loner. For some, this means a move from the absolute to the authentic. It means taking into account contemporary emphasis on tolerance; it means not telling others they are wrong."[96]

The sentiment of the 2000 decade was measured by George Barna in a 20 year survey that concluded in 2009. The study demonstrated that "Americans continue to lose confidence in churches and organized religion... 48% of adults and less than half of them have 'a great deal of

---

[96] D. A. Carson, *Becoming Conversant with the Emerging Church* (Grand Rapids: Zondervan, 2005), 29.

confidence' or 'quite a lot of confidence in churches.'" [97] Interestingly, reading of the Bible rose to 57% since 2001. Barna interpreted these findings as the following "I attribute it to a central finding in the **Maximum Faith** research showing that many ask for God's forgiveness but few are willing to suffer and sacrifice in order to be broken of sin and move on to a life of surrender and submission that produces a deeper relationship with God and a genuine love for other people." [98] The findings reflect the attitude of the times as the prevailing perspective and the way reality is viewed. To humble oneself would be an admission of surrender and servitude to an authoritative figure. This is no longer necessary. What is necessary is to live an "authentic life."

Charles Spurgeon, a fervent and godly preacher during the mid-1800's would have regarded the results of the study as a symptom of "easy-believerism."[99] He states, "I cannot conceive it possible for any one truly to recognize Christ as Savior and yet not to receive Him as Lord."[100] To Spurgeon, one of the prerequisite to salvation is to humble yourself before the Lord, Jesus Christ. He continues, "If Christ is to be yours today you must let Him have dominion over you. 'He must reign.' He claims to be Master and Lord to those who ask salvation at His hands...

---

[97] www.georgebarna.com/2011/08/comments-on-the-august-4-barna-update-"barna-study-of-religious-since-1991-shows-significant-change-by-faith-group.
[98] Ibid.
[99] Steven Lawson, *The Gospel Focus of Charles Spurgeon* (Sanford: Reformation Trust Publisher, 2012), 100
[100] Ibid., 99.

It must be so, or salvation is impossible; those who serve sin are not saved, nor can they be except by being brought to serve the Christ of God."[101]

Scripture states, *"For the mind that is set on the flesh is hostile to God, for it does not submit to God's law, indeed, it cannot"* Rom. 8:7. *"For being ignorant of the righteousness of God, and seeking to establish their own, they did not submit to God's righteousness"* Rom. 10:3. *"Submit yourselves therefore to God. Resist the devil and he will flee from you"* James 4:7.

The last verse is tantamount. It commands us to submit to God for it is the only way to resist Satan and overt self-destruction. Scripture illustrates this in the book of Luke where Satan is trying to tempt Jesus. As it turned out, Satan left after he was reproved by Jesus (Luke 4: 1-13). Are we submitting to God today? In a similar study conducted by the Barna Group the same sample questions were asked to ascertain belief shifts. Certain points surfaced. Although beliefs did not show to change, behaviors of people did. Barna made a startling remark. He states, "Because we know that behavior follows beliefs, we could have anticipated the behavior changes three or four decades ago when there was major upheaval in our belief systems.

The seeds that were sown in the 60's have now been borne through their fruit; decreases in church attendance,

---

[101] Ibid., 99-100.

Sunday school participation, Bible reading and church volunteerism."[102] Seven out of ten maintained an orthodox stance of the "nature of God" but this started to wane after 2001. The belief in the inerrancy of the Bible was also eroding. "If existing tendencies continue, then we will see an increase in the number of people who do not accept a conventional definition of God's character and those who reject the accuracy of the principles taught in the Scriptures." [103] Could these occurrences been prevented if the churches were proactive in defending the faith?

The opposition was formidable. Several popular philosophers who were adherents to the antithesis of deconstruction continued to fan the flames. They were Michael Foucault (1926-1984), a French philosopher who was greatly influenced by Nietzsche. His writings as a social theorist focused on knowledge, power and reasoning/logic and were highly regarded in academia.

Jacques Derrida (1930-2004), another French philosopher and who is commonly associated as the father of deconstruction (although he has denied the connection). He exerted great influence in social sciences, ethics, hermeneutics, ontology, epistemology, aesthetics, and the philosophy of language. A third French philosopher, Jean-Francois Lyotard (1924-1998) was a professor of Critical Theory at the University of California, Irvine. He was an ardent opponent to any universal concept. The last

---

[102]www.georgebarna.com/2011/07/comments-on-the-july-26-barna-update-"barna-examines-trends- in-14-religious-factors-over-20-years.
[103] Ibid.

philosopher whose works influenced the early 21st century was the American philosopher, Richard Rorty (1931-2007). He was known as a postmodern deconstructionist philosopher. At this point, what were the mainline churches doing during this decade. How did they respond?

The Churches

In a captivating biographical book by Eric Metaxas entitled, "*Bonhoeffer. Pastor, Martyr, Prophet, Spy. A Righteous Gentile vs. The Third Reich*, Metaxas not only notes the life of Bonhoeffer during WWII, he also highlights the web of deception in the form of Nazism and its impact on the churches. He writes, "How the German Christians justified trusting and binding the traditionally accepted means of the Scriptures and the doctrine of the church is complicated… inevitably [confusion] arises when the Christian faith becomes too closely related to a cultural or national identity. For many Germans, their national identity had become so melted together with whatever Lutheran Christian faith they had that it was impossible to see either clearly. After 400 years of taking for granted that all Germany were Lutheran Christians, no one really knew what Christianity was anymore."[104]

One wonders today what the future holds for mankind. To get a clue look backwards towards the past, at the events that took place during WWII. The struggles of

---

[104] Eric Metaxas, *Bonhoeffer. Pastor, Martyr, Prophet, Spy* (Nashville: Thomas Nelson, 2010), 174.

the German Protestant church during WWII holds the key to what may lie ahead for the churches today. By God's grace, there were champion pastors like Dietrich Bonhoeffer who risked their lives to hold the line for fundamental Christian doctrines.[105] Are there any champion pastors today who are willing to do the same?

In the most recent decades, conservative or orthodox Christianity is perceived as an old dried up sponge, worthless as it is no longer contributes anything to today's world. Along comes the antithesis of deconstruction. To the ones contemplating the fate of the old dried up sponge of Christianity, deconstruction is considered as the water to revitalize it. When water is applied to the dry sponge one could see and feel the sponge getting wet. As the water continues to be poured on the dry sponge the areas of less saturation gradually become more soaked. Such is the action of deconstruction in Christian theology. As deconstruction gains acceptance in Christian theology, its destructive course seeps into Christianity with intent to saturate it. Attitudes begin to change.

Today the changes are embodied in the Emergent Church Movement (ECM). Mark Driscoll pastor of Mars Hill Church in Seattle, Washington and former adherent to ECM states, "The emergent church is the latest version of liberalism. The only difference is that the old liberalism accompanied modernity and the new liberalism

---

[105] Another good book regarding the Christian churches' struggle during WWII is by Erwin Lutzer, *Hitler's Cross: The Revealing Story of How the Cross of Christ was Used as a Symbol of the Nazi Agenda* (Chicago: Moody Publisher, 1995).

accompanies postmodernism. The emergent or emerging church movement seeks to contextualize the gospel to current postmodern sentiment. There is also the Emergent organization that embodies all that postmodernism has to offer and utilized in their churches."[106]

If we were to compare ECM to the saturation levels of the old dry sponge, we find three levels of dispersion. Delineated by Ed Stetzer in an article found the 2008 Fall edition of "The Journal for Baptist Theology and Ministry" the saturation areas "represent three categories of people that adhere to the ECM." The first category is what he describes as the "Relevants." These are people who are the least influenced with deconstruction. According to Stetzer, "These people attempt to contextualize music, worship, and outreach much like the 'contemporary church' movement of the 1980's-1990's. Their methodology may be considered progressive. However, their theology is often conservative and evangelical. Many are doctrinally sound, growing and impacting lostness."[107]

The second category of people are the ones moderately saturated with deconstruction- the Reconstructionists. "Largely concerned about existing church structures, these people emphasize an 'incarnational' model and may find a home in the house church movement. My main concern with this group has

---

[106] Mark Driscoll, *Confessions of a Reformission Relationship* (Grand Rapids: Zondervan, 2006), 21.

[107] Ed Stetzer, "The Emergent/Emerging Church: A Missiological Perspective" in *The Journal for Baptist Theology and Ministry* Vol. 5 No. 2 Fall, 2008.

been noted. If reconstructionists simply rearrange dissatisfied Christians and do not impact lostness, it is hardly a better situation than the current one. The move appears to be one step beyond the Relevants who maintain existing structures while innovating in worship and outreach."[108]

The third of people would correspond as being fully saturated with the antithesis of deconstruction and are the most controversial. They are the "Revisionists." As Stetzer explains, "For this group, both methodology and theology may be re-visioned. My concerns include that some might dispense with the substitutionary atonement, the reality of hell, views of gender, and the very nature of the Gospel. It is at this point that many believe the move is similar to the mainline churches years ago and I agree."

The last group includes members like Tony Jones, Doug Pagitt, Tim Keil, Chris Senz, Mark Oestreicher, Donald Miller, Leonard Sweet, Spencer Burke, Rob Bell, and Brian McLaren. From these men, Brian McLaren has been the most out spoken and prominent leader. Rob Bell recently published a best seller book, "Love Wins." It was listed in Times Magazine's year in review edition 2011 as one of the top 2011 best seller books. It makes one wonder what is so special about the book that it has reached such heights of popularity.

---

[108] Stetzer, "The Emergent/Emerging Church: A Missiological Perspective" in *The Journal for Baptist Theology and Ministry* Vol. 5 No. 2 Fall, 2008.

For the ECM the sacredness of Scripture does not prevent its deconstruction. In an article entitled, "An Emerging Church Primer," author, Justin Taylor states, "My major concern about what I see in Emergents can be boiled down to four issues: (1) the authority of God's Word; (2) the cross of Christ; (3) the concepts of truth and (4) sexual ethics."[109]

Brian McLaren's thoughts on the inerrancy of the Bible and the play on words is evident as he questions the veracity of the Bible and its inherent messages of God. His questions aim first with the way we have been traditionally taught. He states, "That oft-quoted passage in second Tim [2Tim 3:16] doesn't say 'All Scripture is inspired by God and its *authoritative!* It says that Scripture is inspired and *useful-* useful to teach, rebuke, correct, instruct us to live justly and equip us for our mission as the people of God... We want it to be God's instruction encyclopedia, God's rule book, God's answer book, God's scientific text, God's easy step instruction book, God's little book of morals for all occasions. The only people in Jesus' day who would have had anything close to these expectations of the Bible would have been the scribes and Pharisees. Right?"[110]

To the unsuspecting Christian or the new Christian, McLaren's explanation sounds good but the important

[109] Justin Taylor, "An Emerging Church Primer" www.9marks.org/CC/Article/0,,PTID314526%7CCHD598014%7CCIIDD2249226,00.html.
[110] McLaren, *A New Kind of Christianity,* 74. Proponents of ECM rarely quote Scripture. They speak in generalities.

details such as the authority of God is left out. Taylor likens this attitude in the following statement, "Remember how the serpent led Eve into disobedience: 'Did God actually say, *'You shall not eat of any tree in the garden?'* (Gen. 3:1) Satan does not begin by lying, per se, but with a question. He plants a seed of doubt. 'Hey, I'm asking questions. Raising the issues. Exploring new terrain. I'm not saying God didn't say this. I'm saying just wondering if we all really understood what he said.'" [111]

The second area of concern according to Taylor is the cross of Christ. ECM adherents have a problem with the atoning work of Jesus through penal substitution. ECM's contention is there is not only one way to look at penal substitutionary atonement. Deconstruction of the Gospel and the rebuilding it ala ECM reveals that the cross of Christ is merely a symbol for moral living. Read Rob Bell's critical stance regarding Jesus' work. "The real issue, the one that can't be avoided is whether a person has a 'personal relationship' with God through Jesus. However, that happens whoever told whomever, however it was done, that's the bottom line; a personal relationship. If you don't have that you will die apart from God and spend eternity in torment in hell. The problem, however, is that the phrase 'personal relationship' is found nowhere in the Bible.

Nowhere in the Hebrew scriptures, nowhere in the New Testament. Jesus never used the phrase. Paul didn't

---

[111] Taylor, "An Emerging Church Primer," www.9marks.org/CC/Article/O,PTID314526%7CCHD598014%7CCIIDD2249226,00.html.

use it. Nor did John, Peter, James, or the *woman*[112] who wrote the Letter to the Hebrews. So if that's it, if that's the point of it all, if that's the ticket, the center, the one unavoidable reality the heart of the Christian faith, why is it that no one used the phrase until the last hundred years or so?"[113] Such questioning by Bell is as "just wondering, just raising the issue" sounds familiar like what the serpent was verbalizing to Eve.

In the book, "Why We're Not Emergents," the authors, Kevin DeYoung and Ted Kluck discuss this issue. "Jesus died for many reasons. Or to put it another way, the death of Jesus accomplished many things... John Piper lists 50 reasons why Christ suffered and died. Every reason is supported by explicit texts from the Bible. Piper shows that what Jesus did to show His love to us (Eph. 5:2,25: Gal. 2:20), to destroy hostility between races (Eph. 2:14-16), and to create a people passionate for good works (Titus 2:14).

Jesus also died to restore us from final judgment (Heb. 9:28), to provide the basis for our justification (Rom. 3:24, 28, 5:9), and complete the obedience that becomes our righteousness (Phil. 2:8, 3:9: Rom. 5:19; 2 Cor. 5:21). None of the 50 reasons should be ignored, especially the first one:

---

[112] My emphasis. Most Bible scholars believe that the book of Hebrews may have been written by Barnabas, Paul, Luke as well as Clement or Apollos. Since there is no clear consensus, the author of Hebrews remains anonymous. I highly doubt that the author was a woman since most women were not educated during that period of time. Also, there are no manuscripts or documents from the era written by women that the Book of Hebrew can be compared with to identify its possible female authorship.
[113] Rob Bell, *Love Wins* (New York: HarperOne, 2011), 10-11.

Christ suffered and died to absorb the wrath of God."[114] To agree to other views than what is embodied in the doctrine of penal substitutionary atonement guts the heart of the Gospel.

The third area of concern according to Taylor is truth and knowledge. To the Emergents, truth and knowledge do exist but are viewed differently than what is expected. "While *truth itself* might be changing, our *knowledge of the truth* can never be certain. We have confidence that something is true, but we can never have certainty."[115] For one to "know truth", one has to experience truth. For ECM, experiencing truth is "a spiritual thing... it's a part of the reconnection that is at the heart of true religion; we reconnect with God, with our own soul, with our neighbor, and with all of God's creatures- brother sun, sister moon, and brother dolphin, too." [116] Thus, truth and knowledge as an undeniable absolute, as contained in Scripture, is redefined to mean whatever an individual experiences in relation to his environment. How is this assertion to be applied to the Gospel? For the ECM, the Gospel or the Good News starts as, "It begins with the sure and certain truth that we are loved. That in spite of whatever has gone horribly wrong deep in our hearts and has spread to every corner of the world, in spite of our sins,

---

[114] Kevin DeYoung and Ted Kluck, *Why We're Not Emergent* (Chicago: Moody Publisher, 2008), 192.
[115] Taylor, "An Emerging Church Primer," www.9marks.org/CC/Article/O,PTID314526%7CCHD598014%7CCIIDD2249226,00.html.
[116] McLaren, *A New Kind of Christianity*, 170.

failures, rebellion, and hard hearts, in spite of what's been done to us or what we've done, God has made peace with us. Done. Complete. As Jesus said, 'It is finished.' We are now invited to live a whole new life without guilt or shame or blame or anxiety. We are going to be fine. Of all the conceptions of the divine, or all the language Jesus could put on the lips of the God character in this story he tells, that's what he has the father say."[117]

Kevin DeYoung and Ted Kluck illustrate the ECM contentions as, "'All we need is Jesus,' many emerging Christians cry, 'not these fancy theologies and doctrinal foundations. Thus, Ervin McManus writes, 'The power of the gospel is the result of a person – Jesus Christ- not the message. The gospel is an event to be proclaimed, not a doctrine to be preserved.' Granted this sounds good, and McManus may mean something good by it. But the argument is one sided. How is the gospel event we proclaim different from a message? And how is a message about Jesus – say, who He is and what He did on earth – different than a doctrine?

We can tell people about Jesus every day until He returns again, but without some doctrinal content filling up what we mean by Jesus and why he matters, we are just shouting slogans, not proclaiming any kind of intelligent gospel."[118] Reducing Scripture to tales or narratives as stated by Taylor, "they [ECM proponents] are able to

---

[117] DeYoung and Kluck, *Why We're Not Emergent,* 108.
[118] Ibid.

discuss 'the big picture,'- broad trajectories, themes, and metaphors- without digging into the details. But God has given us the details of Scripture for a reason. Not a word is wasted in our Bible."[119] It seems that deconstruction has pulled apart the "Good News" and reconstructed it to mean just an event. How pathetic.

The fourth and last area of concern is sexual ethics. In regards to homosexuality, ECM has taken a stance of ambiguity. As stated by McLaren, "We've heard all sides but no position has yet won our confidence so that we say, 'it seems good to the Holy Spirit and us.'" [120] What more proof does one need! Scripture does not mince words! The Lord is very clear on His thoughts regarding sexual morality as stated in the previous chapter.

Conclusion

With the church being weak to stand firm as secular winds of change blow, the antithesis of the decade prevails. So much so that theology is saturated with it resulting in secularism interpreting Scripture. Exposed in the book of Revelation are seven churches as representatives of all churches. These churches were assaulted with false teachings, cultural pressure to conform to society, materialism and persecution. The battle was a spiritual one

---

[119] Taylor, "An Emerging Church Primer," www.9marks.org/CC/Article/O,PTID314526%7CCHD598014%7CCIIDD2249226,00.html.
[120] Ibid.

between God and Jesus and Satan and evilness for the soul of the church.

The book's author, John, "warn[s] the church and fortify it to endure suffering and to stay pure from the deviling enticements of the present world order."[121] These words were penned two millennia ago but they still are applicable today. The battle for the soul of the church continues to rage on today. Will the churches heed John's warning? The next chapter discusses man's desire for tangible faith and the strategy to obtain it.

---

[121] *English Standard Version Study Bible* (Wheaton: Crossway, 2008), 2454.

Chapter Nine

✧✧✧

THE QUEST FOR A TANGIBLE FAITH: THE PLAN

"You might be an emergent Christian: if you listen to U2, Moby, and Johnny Cash's *Hurt* (sometimes in church), use sermon illustrations from *The Sopranos,* drink lattes in the afternoon and Guinness in the evenings, and always use a Mac; if you're reading list consists primarily of Stanley Hauerwas, Henri Nouwen, N. T. Wright, Stan Grenz, Dallas Willard, Brennan Manning, Jim Wallis, Fredereick Buechner, David Bosch, John Howard Yoder, Wendall Berry, Nancy Murphy, John Franke, Walter Winks, and Leslie Newbigin (not to mention McLaren, Pagitt, Bell, etc.) and your sparring partners include D. A. Carson, John Calvin, Martyn Lloyd-Jones, and Wayne Grudem; if your idea of quintessential Christian discipleship is Mother Teresa, Martin Luther King, Jr., Nelson Mandela, or Desmond Tutu; if you don't like George W. Bush or institutions or big business or capitalism, or *Left Behind* Christianity; if your political concerns over poverty, AIDS, imperialism, war-mongering, CEO salaries, consumerism, global warming, racism, and oppression and not so much abortion and gay marriage; if you are into bohemian, goth, rave, or indie; if you lie awake at night having nightmares about all the ways modernism has ruined your life; if you love the Bible as a beautiful, inspiring collection of words that lead us into the mystery of God but is not inerrant; if you search for truth but aren't sure it can be found; if you've ever been to a church with prayer labyrinths, candles, Play-Doh, chalk drawings, couches, or beanbags (your youth group doesn't count); if you loathe words like *linear, propositional, rational, machine,* and *hierarchy* and use words like *ancient-future, jazz, mosaic, matrix, missional, vintage,* and *dance*; if you grew up in a very conservative Christian home that in retrospect seems legalistic, naïve, and rigid; if you support women in all levels of ministry; prioritize urban over suburban, and like your theology narrative instead of systematic; if you disbelieve in any sacred-secular divide; if you want to be the church and not just go to the church; if you long for a community that is relational, tribal, and primal like a river or a garden; if you believe doctrine gets in the way of an interactive relationship with Jesus; if you believe who goes to hell is no one's business and no one may be there anyway; if you believe salvation has a little to do with atoning for guilt and a lot to do with bringing the whole creation back into shalom with its Maker; if you believe following Jesus is not believing the right things but living the right way; if it really bugs you when people talk about going to heaven instead of heaven coming to us; if you disdain monological, didactic preaching; if you use the word 'story' in all your propositions about postmodernism - if all or most of this tortuously long sentence describes you, then you might be an emergent Christian."[122]

McLaren writes in one of his books, "Modernity only wants abstract principles, universal concepts and disembodied absolutes. So we take an expression like 'the kingdom of God' and try to give it meaning without context. Postmodern theology has to reincarnate; we have to get back into the flesh and blood and sweat and dirt of the setting, because as I said, all truth is contextual. If the Bible teaches anything, it teaches that. After all, there's no 'First, Second, and Third Trinity' or 'Book of Moral Absolutes' or anything like that. Instead there are letters and prophecies, all with a specific address, a specific time, a specific context. The word of the Lord always comes to a specific somebody, in a specific somewhere, at some specific time. But with the kingdom, we've only scratched the surface of all meaning that's there."[123]

Over the last twenty years discontent with the way of "doing church" has led to the scrutiny of mainline churches as well as the evangelical ones. Presently, Diana Butler-Bass, Ph.D., fellow at Seabury-Western Theological Seminary has gone as far as to state that mainline churches

[122] DeYoung and Kluck, *Why We're Not Emergent*, 20-22.
[123] McLaren, *A New Kind of Christianity*, 152.

are dead. The dissatisfaction voiced towards "institutional"churches provides an avenue to an ecclesial re-vision. Together with the ECM, the postmodern era present a new way of interpreting Christianity.

Such articulated ideology may be passed off as a fad of the day. But the opposite is true. The manifestation of a "new" Christianity will demonstrate itself as, "The expression of ideas assimilated into a variety of denominations, and so in many ways theological constructs. The breadth of the Emergent Church ethos found in nearly every denominational setting makes it hard to consider the movement expressly theological. It may very well lead to 're-visionary' theological formulations, but this approach often be done so on the context of one's faith tradition."[124] The plan to transition churches away from traditional, conservative foundations of Christianity to a postmodern church that embraces the emergent church philosophy is well underway.

The Plan

The plan initially targets the seminaries where the future church leaders, the pastors as the shepherds of God's flock are trained. The goal for the seminaries is two - fold. First, "dethrone theoretical knowledge... The dethroning of theoretical knowledge will require something far more

[124] Stetzer, "The Emergent/Emerging Church: A Missiological Perspective" in *The Journal for Baptist Theology and Ministry* Vol. 5 No. 2 Fall, 2008.

radical than rewriting seminary curricula; it will require reinventing the whole idea of professional ministry training. It might even make us deconstruct the idea of professional."[125]

Usurping theoretical knowledge in seminaries is accomplished by advocating practice or orthopraxy over doctrinal knowledge or orthodoxy. The inverted logic believes that, "How a person lives is more important than *what he or she believes.*"[126] Matt. 25:31-46 is used to substantiate this claim where the verse depicts Jesus rewarding those who help the poor and needy. Matt. 7:24-27 is additionally pointed out to prove that Jesus himself states that a true believer does His works. The focal point is shifted from faith in Jesus and His atoning death and resurrection, the indwelling Holy Spirit and the resultant works that glorify His Name. Instead the focus is one that reflects living and doing as Jesus would want.

The second goal for seminaries is to modify practicum to include a monastic experience and become more missional in scope. ECM's answer for a tangible Christianity is found in a monastic lifestyle. In a quest for knowledge in order to build spirituality, the thought is to reach back into the past before the Reformation initiated by Martin Luther in the 16th century.

---

[125] McLaren, *A New Kind of Christianity,* 209.
[126] Scot McKnight, "Five Streams of the Emerging Church."
www.christianitytoday.com/ct/2007/february/11.35html.

ECM wants to revive communal living, shared living and spiritual "practices." The hope is to transcend traditional churches; that is, Bible studies, prayer groups, Sunday school to a more enlightening experience. The new concept takes on a Roman Catholic and Eastern Orthodox flavor in the form of symbols, sacraments, special candles, incense, contemplative prayers, piety through works, and promotion of mysticism. An example of a practice would be breath prayers where a short verse or a single word is repeated with each breath.

Including a missional component to seminaries is not a bad idea. Students go out into the field and visit various community projects such as youth camps, community facilities, church planting, and church internships here and abroad. The mission's focus would be to make "agents for God's kingdom." But how would these agents serve God in a tangible faith? According to McLaren, missions are to change from its traditional perspective of winning souls for Christ. His sentiment about missions is as the following, "Although I don't hope that Buddhists will become (cultural) Christians, I do hope all who feel so called will become Buddhists followers of Jesus; I believe they should be given that opportunity and invitation. I don't hope all Jews or Hindus will become members of the Christian religion. But I do hope all who feel so called will become Jewish or Hindu followers of Jesus."[127] The missional task according to McLaren is not to bring the Word of God to the lost and dying in sin but to

---

[127] Brian McLaren, *A Generous Orthodoxy* (Grand Rapid: Zondervan, 2004), 113.

bless everyone. Truth deconstructed once again and in direct opposition to Matt 28:19 where it states, *"go therefore and make disciples of all nations, baptizing them to observe all that I have commanded you. And behold, I am with you always, to the end of time."*

The second part of the plan is to transform churches to a "new" philosophy of ministering. The new philosophy of ministering contains three interrelating aspects. They are community, spirituality, and missions. The overarching purpose of the church will change from one of its traditional responsibility "to equip its members for the benefit of the world."[128] An endeavor as this would look like the following. "A quick read through the *Grand Rapids Press* Religion section (February 10, 2007) is telling. There is a breathily written article entitled 'Church More Spiritual Than Religious,' in which the author describes the '10:03' service at 'The Journey,' a new Grand Rapids downtown church located-you guessed it-in a renovated factory building right next to a coffee shop. The church, started by Bill Freeman, a former television news reporter and radio-show host, will feature 'songs heard on mainstream' radio such as U2's 'Still Haven't Found What I'm Looking For,' which may be the most over-ridden pony in the entire emergent movement.

The sermons are going to be based on the Bible, but they will also use other sacred sources such as the Quran or something that Ghandi or the Dalai Lama said, explains

---

[128] Brian McLaren, *A New Kind of Christian*, 222.

Freeman in the piece, written as though it is seeing the anti-establishment church-in-jeans model explained for the first time. 'So it's Bible plus.' Freeman added that he will encourage a 'sermon-as-discussion' format, and goes on to say that he will try to make space look 'kind of night clubby like a comedy club.' He also intends, for the record, on wearing jeans and a sport coat." [129]

The new church ministry will also entail reaching out to the existing congregation of a church. They would have to buy into the new way of doing church. McLaren states that this too, has a strategy. He remarks, "We create a place of belonging, where people can learn to believe the good news, belong to a community that is learning to behave (or live) by it, and become (together) a living example of it."[130] The Plan continues with addressing the issue of congregation participation. Two radical strategies are offered. "First, you can push down the status quo-scare people; help them see that things aren't as copasetic as they believe them to be. Second, you can lift up a vision-inspire people, help them see that things could be so much better. There's a place for both, but without the second, the first is only a short-term quick-fix tool for change…plan to lead by no more than 25% status quo redefinition [deconstruction] and at least 75% vision inspiration."[131]

The church is certainly a place where we come together as the Body of Christ. We belong together in the

[129] DeYoung and Kluck, *Why We're Not Emergent*, 212.
[130] McLaren, *A New Kind of Christianity*, 222.
[131] McLaren, *A New Kind of Christianity*, 212-213.

concrete sense such as being together in a physical location but we also share fellowship because of a spiritual bond that unites us in Christ. Compare McLaren's tactics to Bonhoeffer's. Dietrich Bonhoeffer explains, "Christianity means community through Jesus Christ and in Jesus Christ no Christian community is more or less than this. Whether it be a brief, single encounter or the daily fellowship of years, Christian community is only this. We belong to one another through and in Jesus Christ."[132]

The concept of church community also involves the Holy Spirit who was sent to us by Jesus Christ after His ascension and who reveals to us God's will so we will be of one accord (Cor. 12:13). Contrast that with the ECM's definition of Christian community where "**people learn to believe**" and "**learning to behave.**" Somewhat contradictory in a movement's search to be more spiritual, that actions involve works, performed by oneself. It flies in the face of God's grace, the free gift of faith that begins our relationship with Jesus. How about the work of Jesus and the work of the Holy Spirit? It seems that in the quest for tangible faith, key Biblical truths are discarded by the wayside.

Spirituality is the next component in a new philosophy of church ministry. McLaren states, "Spirituality focuses on the 'holy' part. But it is not just about individual spirituality (as was the case of modernity,

---

[132] Dietrich Bonheoffer, *Life Together* (New York: Harper Row Publishers, 1954), 21. I Highly recommend this book for the study of Christian community.

where everything was privatized, atomized, individualized). The spirituality itself is communal. True, the 'done in secret' part is important, but what we experience with God in secret must be brought to the community and shared like a common meal. So we read the Bible as a community, always listening for the insights and input of others. We pray as a community, our individual prayers merging with those of our brothers and sisters. We fast and study and celebrate and worship and rest together. In these ways, through private and communal spiritual disciplines, we become unique, holy people."[133]

The ECM "spirituality" that is pursued according to David Wells is, "not seeking the God of the Christian religion, who is transcendent, who speaks to life from outside of it and entered it through the Incarnation, whose word is absolute and enduring, and whose moral character defines the difference between Good and Evil forever. Rather, it is the god within, the god who is found within the self and in whom the self is rooted."[134] Wells continues, "The premise beneath all of these spiritualities is that sin has not intruded upon the relation between the sacred and human nature, that human nature itself offers access- indeed, we assume, unblemished access- to God, that human nature itself mediates the divine. Gone are the days when people understood that an avalanche has fallen between God and human beings, that human nature retains

---

[133] McLaren, *A New Kind of Christianity*, 223.
[134] David Wells in "The Supremacy of Jesus Christ in a Postmodern World" www.desiringGod.org, 36. A free download and a highly recommended read.

its shape as made in the image of God but has lost its membership to God and stands in pained alienation from him."[135]

A "spiritual" person according to the Apostle Paul is one that is led by the Holy Spirit. As stated in 1Cor. 2:7,10, 13, *"But we impart a secret and hidden wisdom of God, which God decreed before the ages of our glory…these things God has revealed to us through the Spirit. For the Spirit searches everything, even the depths of God…And we impart this in words not taught by human wisdom but taught by the Spirit interpreting spiritual truths to those who are spiritual."*

The third component of the Plan to transform the churches is in the area of missions. Missions or missionology of the churches is not seen as the means to an end but only as a "catalyst." The purpose of mission via the church is not to bring people to Jesus but solely to serve the people. The goal of which is to seek to "serve by loving and living in such a way that we bless those around us. But more that, we are to be engaged in changing and even creating culture as we bring the kingdom of God to earth. Rather than calling out of the world system and into *'the kingdom of His beloved Son'* (Col. 1:13, NASB), we are to bring the kingdom to them."[136]

---

[135] Wells in "The Supremacy of Jesus Christ in a Postmodern World" www.desiringGod.org, 36.

[136] Gary Gilley in *Reforming or Conforming? Post – Conservative Evangelicals and the Emergent Church* (Wheaton: Crossway Books, 2008), 287.

Rob Bell writes, "For Jesus, the question wasn't how do I get into Heaven? But how do I bring heaven here?... The goal isn't escaping this world but making this world the kind of place God can come to. And God is remaking us into the kind of people who can do this work."[137] For Bell the kingdom of God is already here. But what does Jesus say about the kingdom in John 18:36? He states, *"My kingdom is not of this world."* In Isa. 52:11 and repeated in 2Cor. 6:17 by Paul who states, *"Therefore go out from their midst, and be separate from them, says the Lord, and touch no unclean thing; then I will welcome you."*

A call from God is to separate ourselves from the sinful world. Do not partake in it. Why? 1 John 2:15-17 explains, *"Do not love the world or the things in the world. If anyone loves the world, the love of the Father is not in him. For all that is in the world-the desires of the flesh and the desires of the eyes and pride in possessions-is not from the Father but is from the world. And the world is passing away along with its desires, but whoever does the will of God abides forever."*

Translated into current conservatives' perspective, Dr. Gary Gilley opines on the ECM stance by stating, "Half truths twisted into distorted vision. Did Jesus show compassion and minister to the poor? Certainly. Did Jesus, or the apostles after him fight for social justice on behalf of the poor and needy? Not at all. While Jesus, through the transformation of lives, began a process that

---

[137] RobBell, *Love Wins* (New York: HarperOne, 2011), 40.

would revolutionize much of the world in regard to injustice, he never made these things a central platform of his ministry or that of the church."[138]

The church is expected to go to the masses for the sole purpose of reaching them. But to change the purpose that which it is ordained to do, which is to bring people out of the darkness of sin into the light of God is blatantly wrong! ECM's mission is to prevent injustice is hypocritical! The grave injustice is committed when the Truth is withheld from the people, specifically the atonement of Jesus Christ! The Lord makes it very clear in Rom. 1:18-20 where it states, *"For the wrath of God is revealed from heaven against all ungodliness and unrighteousness, who by their unrighteous suppress the truth. For what can be known of God is plain to them, because God has shown it to them. For his invisible attributes, namely, his eternal power and divine nature, have been clearly perceived, ever since the creation of the world, in the things that have been made. So they are without excuse."*

Bringing these changes into the church requires a carefully planned strategy. "The other big decision is bringing about change, but especially in a church, is whether to move incrementally or innovately. Incremental changes (improving little by little) are great when your basic system is sound but…incremental change is the worst enemy of true innovation. Innovation means introducing a

---

[138] Gary Gilley in *Reforming or Conforming? Post – Conservative Evangelicals and the Emergent Church* (Wheaton: Crossway Books, 2008), 287.

bold new system, a new philosophy. A whole new plan…Maybe you do both-create incremental improvement of your existing services and at the same time innovate by creating new ways of 'doing business.' What that would mean in church transition would be this: you would lead a revolution by addition, not subtraction. You wouldn't change the 'services'…so loved by your dominant group. But you would for all new worship and spiritual growth experiences for new people-completely new ways of doing things."[139]

An example of a strategy for change is the following. "I would lean toward maximizing rather than minimizing discontinuity. In other words, don't try to underestimate how significant the changes are to the people. Instead, tell them, 'I'd like us to consider making some really major and difficult changes in the way we do ministry around here.' If I were assigned to a struggling church, I might propose that they actually shut down the church but stay together as a core group to plan a new beginning. Then I'd help them chose a new name, symbolic of a whole new philosophy of ministry that we would develop. I would also bring in a lot of outside consultants. Outsiders have so much more power than insiders-another counterintuitive reality I've discovered."[140]

[139] Ibid., 213-214.
[140] McLaren, *A New Kind of Christianity,* 214.

The Lord's response as stated in Scripture:

Matt. 7:15: *"Beware of false prophets, who come to you in sheep's clothing but inwardly are ravenous wolves."*

Lam. 2:14: *"Your prophets have seen for you false and deceptive visions; they have not exposed your iniquity to restore your fortunes, but have seen for you oracles that are false and misleading."*

Eze. 13:9-10: *My hand will be against the prophet who see false visions and who give lying divinations. They shall not be in the council of my people nor be enrolled in the register of the house of Israel. And you shall know that I am Lord GOD. Precisely because, they have misled my people saying, 'Peace, when there is no peace, and because, when the people build a wall, these prophets smear it with whitewash."*

Conclusion

Knowledge of Scripture is the only way one can discern what is of God. We are easily deceived when wolves dressed in sheep's clothing come into society speaking words we are familiar with (such as church, mission, peace, spirituality). These words are also found in Scripture but their meanings perverted. As it states in Ps. 44:22, *"we are regarded as sheep to be slaughtered,"* and stated in Isa. 53:6, *"all we like sheep have gone astray; we have turned everyone to his own way."*

The progression of secular thought, now seeped in Hegelian logic has eroded our Christian paradigm of logic. Isa. 1:22 describes how our logic has become, *"Your silver has become like dross, your best wine mixed with water."* We are no longer in line with God's logic. It has been tainted and if we are not careful, just like silver and wine, will eventually be spoiled beyond repair.

Deconstruction conjures mental images of breaking something apart, the act of separating. It continues to separate us from God. The Body of Christ will be led to a Christless faith if deconstruction continues unchecked. We must remember what the Lord explicitly <u>commands,</u> *"You shall not add to the word that I command you, nor take from it, that you may keep the commandments of the Lord your God that I command you"* (Deut. 4:2).

But as detailed in the next chapter, man does not take heed. The proponents of ECM were given a gift to lead people to the truth of Christ and knowledge of God. Their gift lies in the ability to communicate to people across all generations. Their mode of explanation is engaging and convincing. The divine purpose of the gift is to present the Truth to all nations of people. As documented, the case does not exist. ECM creates a master plan to usher in a new church in the 21st century with a new body of worshippers- "the new people" that are not in alliance with God. The Lord warns the proponents of falsehood in 1Cor. 8:9, *"But take care that this right of yours does not somehow become a stumbling block to the weak. For if anyone sees you who have knowledge eating in an idol's temple, will he not be encouraged, if his conscience is weak, to eat food offered to idols? And so by your knowledge this weak person is destroyed, the brother for whom Christ died."*

Need more evidence? Read on. The next chapter entitled, "The Main Thing is no longer the Main Thing" details the erosion taking place in churches.

Chapter Ten

❧❧❧

"The Main Thing is no longer the Main Thing"

"**D**ale Van Dyke, pastor of Harvest Orthodox Presbyterian Church in suburban Grand Rapids, looks not unlike Rick Moranis, circa *Honey, I Shrunk the Kids*...To say that Van Dyke's methods, with the youth at least, are unorthodox would be an understatement. He leads a weekly Wednesday night class in which twenty-five high school students voluntarily read chapters from *Bible Doctrines*, by Wayne Grudem, and answer a series of questions. If they haven't finished the chapter they aren't allowed to attend. This is quite a departure from the usual 'try to be hip enough to get the cool kids to show up and everyone else will follow' model of youth ministry that has provided the spark for emergent movement. 'The kids know that most of the other stuff is fluff,' he says. 'They want truth, and they want to feel like what they're doing is important.' I ask Van Dyke about the emergent assertion that guys like him, with churches like his, are out of touch and culturally irrelevant. 'It sort of makes me laugh,' he says. 'People haven't changed in terms of the reality of the conscience, and the reality of sin, guilt, and fear. Everything that's been the 'issue' since Adam is still the 'issue.' I don't have a problem with asking, 'Are we communicating well?' But I still believe that the preached Word is still God's primary means of communicating with the culture. It's a man set on fire. Give this fifty years and it will be something that you study in your religion history books, but the debris will be all over the place in terms of people who have just absolutely walked away from the church. Van Dyke also addresses the breathless excitement with which some in the emergent movement view what they're doing. The idea that they are ushering in the next great reformation. He is the first to admit that he feels equally passionate and frustrated, which is evident from his comments. 'Leonard Sweet drives me straight up a wall,' he says. 'It's pure historical ignorance…or arrogance. It's as though the church for the last two thousand years hasn't a clue what they're doing, and now, thanks to guys like Sweet, we can start doing church. I read *Soul Tsunami*, where he says, 'God has hit the reset button on the world. What does that mean? Is that so profound?' 'I want to protect my heart, though,' he says. 'I don't want to be arrogant, and I don't want to be angry…' 'I have no problem with the Paul in Athens model of people doing a church a little bit differently to communicate the gospel,' he says. 'But you always need to go back to teaching the gospel, preaching the Word of God, and a vibrant ministry of mercy inside and out. If you're doing that, do it in your living room. I don't have a problem with that.' All these churches now, they're building coffee shops,' he says. 'I love coffee shops! But if you're depending on a coffee shop to bring people in, you've lost it. And all of the marketing quirks that drove us nuts about the church-growth movement will soon begin to drive us nuts about this one. It's still marketing, but to a different demographic. 'The main thing is no longer the main thing.'"[141]

ECM's retort to the traditional way of "doing church" is that it is time to change. In the past the churches for the most part resisted change but what they provided was not enough. As is demonstrated in the previous chapters, changes in the church caused consequences and some backlash. The sequela from church strife has to do with what McLaren contends as, "it's about attitude, theology, and spirituality. If attitudes change, the stylistics are not only easier to change, but they will also 'want' to change."[142] McLaren is absolutely right. If logic, the way one thinks or perceives reality changes, all the other pieces internal and external to the individual will change such as attitude and theology and eventually the way of "doing church." Theology will be perceived as "…not so much as a list of beliefs or an outline of beliefs. It's more of a story, the story of how people have sought and learned about God through the centuries.

[141] DeYoung and Kluck, *Why We're Not Emergent,* 218-219.
[142] McLaren, *A New Kind of Christianity,* 219.

Like any human story, it's got ups and downs, glories and embarrassments. But that's because it's a human story. Of course God is involved - shown both in the glories and embarrassments, the glories given vs. glimpses of God's own glory, and the embarrassments giving us glimpses of God's mercy, patience, and compassion... In some ways, theology is about generating models of the universe that flow from our understanding of God and the story we find ourselves in."[143]

Hegelian logic suits well for McLaren and the ECM. Through Hegelian logic, the change the ECM proponents seek will certainly achieve actualization of their agenda. But what about spirituality? How does Hegelian logic impact spirituality? The desire for spirituality has become the religion of the 21st century.[144] Its objective has dupped society by a process of emphasizing relationships, practices, and experiences that connect people to a supposedly deeper awareness of self and others in a global community. "There are powerful new forces that help the process such as egalitarianism, communalism, environmentalism, economic life, and mutual responsibilities...new forms of compassion toward others and toward the planet...[we] see differently [and]...that reflects a divine dream or reconciliation, peace, dignity, and justice."[145]

Charles Spurgeon once wrote regarding the Holy Spirit and the Word of God. He says, "How often we have

---

[143] McLaren, *A New Kind of Christianity,* 231.
[144] Ibid
[145] Diana Butler Bass, *Christianity After Religion* (New York: HarperOne, 2012), 259.

found our utter inability to understand some part of divine truth. We asked some of God's people, and they helped us a little. But after all, we were not satisfied till we took it to the throne of heavenly grace and implored the teachings of the blessed Spirit. Then how sweetly it was opened to us; we could eat of it spiritually. It was no longer a husk and shell, hard to be understood. It was bread to us, and we could eat to the full."[146]

Spurgeon's depiction of the Holy Spirit and the Word of God is the embodiment of spirituality. In the current postmodern culture, spirituality is defined as "an umbrella word, a catch all concept used to characterize a commitment to the sacred elements of life. It defies a singular definition, hence the fluidity of the word. Spirituality is deemed as an evolving term rather than one of fixed determination, universally signifying a rejection of traditional faiths as a primary source of connection to the divine."[147]

The monstrous error of the new spirituality of the 21st century is that God becomes second place with self as number one. Our fleshly urges are valued above those of the Lord, our God in an effort to quench the thirst of a tangible religion that exalts man. The great lie that blinds

---

[146] Charles Spurgeon, *The Metropolitan Tabernacle Pulpit*, Vol. XI (Pasadena: Pilgrim Publishers, 1979), 286.

[147] Barry Taylor, "Goodbye Religion, Hello Spirituality: Is There a Place for the Christian "Religion" in the 21st Century?

http://blog.christianitytoday.com/ourfor/archives/2007/03/goodbye_religion_l.html.

man is that sin does not tarnish one's relationship with God.

In order to bring about a transition in the churches, there must be leaders to keep the momentum of the change process. According to the ECM, two qualities are required for leaders. They must possess patience and compassion. The plan to deconstruct the churches and the reconstruct them is estimated to take about fifteen to twenty years. It is "a subversive plan to locate and train a new generation of church planters and pastors. On the surface [they] look like a typical wild and crazy youth worker, but underneath [they are] an agent of radical change in the church."[148]

Thus the plan to bring about change in the churches is to literally grow a new generation of churches complete with a new breed of pastors that would usher a "new and refreshed" Christianity. A new generation of churches will fulfill societal need for a tangible yet spiritual religion. One can takes cues from Ancient-Future Theology (AFT) that was founded by Robert E. Webber in 1978. Webber advocated that tangibility and spirituality based on self can be found in the churches first seven century history. AFT's foundational theme is to be "authentic." Authenticity is a premise that is certainly plausible as long as it is true to God's Word and will. But to the deconstructed church,

---

[148] McLaren, *A New Kind of Christianity,* 221.

authenticity means a rejection of individualism in favor of experiencing living and worshipping in a community.[149]

Conclusion

Tumultuous and uncertain times are confronted every day. An increased desire to have peace in one's life parallels the times. Inwardly we know that present day churches are not offering the salve to heal hurt, stress and anxiety. Statistics show the downward trend in church attendance which reflects society's sentiments about church.

What is currently offered in church is a watered down, reconstructed gospel message that appeases, if only momentarily, society's fleshly needs. In a lost and dying (in sin) world, the call for "community" and "spirituality" is an irresistible enticement. There is nothing wrong with the call as long as it is grounded in God's Word. But as demonstrated, God is pushed from the front burner in society to the back burner in favor of self. Diana Butler Bass, an adherent to this new mindset declares, what is currently happening is the "Great Reversal." The Great Reversal becomes the antithesis for the ensuring years of the 21st century.

---

[149] A good book to read and learn more about the consequences of a new breed of pastors and churches is in *Reforming or Conforming? Post-Evangelicals and the Emerging Church* by Gary L. W. Johnson and Ronald N. Gleason, eds. (Wheaton: Crossways Books, 2008).

Chapter Eleven

৵৵৵

"THE GREAT REVERSAL"[150]

"**M**odern man following Hegel, believes only in dialectical process. There is a thesis; it has 'an antithesis.' Neither is true or false. 'Truth' for today lies only in a synthesis. And even that synthesis is not true forever, for tomorrow there will arise another thesis different from today's and out of the combination of these will come 'truth' for tomorrow. But in no case will these 'truths' be absolute."[151]

In a new book, *Christianity After Religion, The End of Church and the Birth of a New Spiritual Awakening,* by Diana Butler Bass, the context of the second decade of the 21st century for the Christian is not receiving eternal life by accepting Jesus Christ as Lord and Savior but celebrating

---

[150] Diana Butler Bass

[151]Francis Schaeffer, The Church at the End of the 20th Century (Downers Grove: Intervarsity Press, 1972) 83-84

our own life. For Bass, to become a Christian, one has to follow the three B's.

They are, in proper order belonging, behaving, and believing. Bass and adherents to ECM believe that the concept "belonging" is the foundation of Christianity. Bass writes, "Christianity did not begin with a confession. It began with an invitation into friendship, into creating a new community ["state" if we use Hegelian political philosophy], into forming relationships based on love and service."[152] "Belonging to a community [state] starts with a flash of recognition, an intuition or connection…our heart leads the way."[153]

The heart is what is thought to start our spiritual awakening, and love expresses itself in relationships and communities. There is truth to the contention that spiritual activity starts in the heart but according to Scripture the heart is also where all actions of human life emanate from. "The heart is also the seat of the conscious (Rom. 2:15). It is naturally wicked (Gen. 8:21), and hence it contaminates the whole life and character of a person (Matt. 12:34; 15:8).[154] Pure love comes from God. He is the source of love. *"For love is from God, and whoever loves has been born of God and knows God. Anyone who does not love does not know God, because God is love"* (1John 4:7-8). The entire Bible speaks of God's love which is pure and perfect.

---

[152] Bass, *Christianity After Religion*, 205.
[153] Ibid.
[154] *Easton Bible Dictionary*, www.biblestudytools.com.

Unlike "natural love [that] is like gold mixed with an abundance of dross. It is tarnished by selfish interests. It is mixed with the lead of envy and the alloys of rudeness. It is an inconsistent love."[155] The call to belong causes confusion when relationships are initiated before one believes. In a secular community one seeks a relationship with another because he/she believes that the other is good to have in their life for whatever reason.

According to Francis Schaeffer, "The Christian community as a community should understand that *its* first relationship is not horizontal, but vertical. The Christian community is made of those who are in a personal relationship with God. Its first job is not toward the lost, though it has a task there. The first thing the Christian community should do is to stand (*as a community*) in a living, existential, moment – by – moment relationship with God. The congregation, the Christian college student body, the family, whatever the community is, this fellowship of believers should stand in awe and worship waiting before God." Jer. 23:10-11 *"For the land is full of adulterers; because of the curse the land mourns; and the pastures of the wilderness are dried up. Their course is evil, and their might is not right. Both prophet and priest are ungodly; even in my house I have found their evil, declares the Lord."*

---

[155] R. C. Sproul, *The Mystery of the Holy Spirit* (Carol Stream: Tyndale House Publishers, 1990), 167-168.

The next "B" is behaving and is interpreted as "right living." Right living is done by imitating Jesus' actions. "Behavior opens the door for believing… with practices, faith is but an empty promise."[156] There is no problem with right living. But when God's incarnation through Jesus Christ is meant solely to "practice faith" because actions shape faith, it becomes a totally different matter.

An argument made by ECM proponents is that just because one believes or has faith does not necessarily make one live a godly life. The recent church scandals are pointed at to lend credence to their argument. The real issue with this argument is whether the Christians involved in scandal were really being led by the guidance and counsel of the indwelling Holy Spirit. The nature and will of God is revealed to us by the Holy Spirit. So far in the first two "B's," belonging and believing the Holy Spirit is not mentioned or given any credit for His role in one's life. Through the Holy Spirit, faith works in us and it manifests outwardly where it is witnessed by others.

Faith is a free gift of God; not something that is acquired by our own doing. God gives it to us and we in turn practice it. "Christian life is not lived rightly without the right beliefs as the foundation. Not every Christian needs to be a seminary- trained theological scholar, but every Christian does need to understand the nature of the God we worship."[157]

---

[156] Bass, *Christianity After Religion,* 208.
[157] Sproul, *The Mystery of the Holy Spirit,* 73.

This leads us to the final step towards becoming a "Christian." The last "B" is believing. How believing happens after belonging and behaving is found in the book of Matthew, according to Bass, "Peter's confession of faith grew out of his friendship with Jesus and the things that they had done together – praying, eating, preaching, healing, giving, and feeding. In the Gospel of Matthew, before Peter's confession of Jesus as the Messiah (16: 13-20), Jesus and his disciples had fed the great crowd that had been following their band (15:32-39). Together, they had practiced hospitality. Before he asks, 'Who do you say that I am?' Jesus reminds them of this act of miraculous hospitality, saying that the action pointed to greater spiritual realities of God's power and presence in the world (16: 8-10).

In response to what he has experienced, Peter blurts out, 'You are the Messiah, the Son of the living God'…Jesus says that Peter's insight comes from God's spirit, not any 'flesh and blood' knowledge… the sort of knowledge that comes from engagement with God, others, and the world. It's a credo."[158] Credo in Latin means "I believe, "referring to a religious belief. The interaction or interplay between our relationship with God, with people and the world shapes our beliefs. Beliefs are thus represented in one's experience.[159]

---

[158] Bass, *Christianity After Religion,* 208-209.
[159] Ibid.

Is this premise correct according to Scripture? Eph. 2: 8-9 states, *"For by grace you have been saved through faith. And this is not of your doing, it is a gift of God not as a result of works so that no one may boast."* In Rom. 3:20, it states, *"For by works of the law no human being will be justified in his sight."* Faith or belief is not based on proof or value of works. It is not earned, merited or arrived at through experience. Our belief comes to us by the grace of God. We cannot in some way cooperate with God in order to bring about our faith/belief. We need God's intervention through grace to save us.

In Eph. 2:5 Paul states, *"Even when we are dead in our trespasses, made us alive together with Christ – by grace have been saved."* Salvation rests solely on God's grace. Human achievement or experiences have nothing to do with faith that leads to salvation.

In the Old Testament and in Jesus' time, one came to faith by the power of the Holy Spirit. "The Spirit must bring about conviction and illumination in the hearts of the converted."[160] Conversion is the exclusive domain of the Holy Spirit. At that point, one embarks on the road of sanctification, by the work of the Holy Spirit within us. What manifests is the fruit of the Holy Spirit, not to be confused with "civil righteousness" or rightful living although one can be kind, thoughtful and generous without having the indwelling Holy Spirit. "External righteous is what outwardly corresponds to the law of God, but lacks

---

[160] Lawson, *The Gospel Focus of Charles Spurgeon*, 119.

the motivation from a heart disposed toward the love of God."[161]

Basically ECM is not concerned with what one believes but is more interested in how one believes. Their contention is, "*What* to *how* is a shift from information about experience *of*. *What* is a conventional religious question, one of dogma and doctrine; *how* is an emerging spiritual question, one of experience and connection. We have lived through many generations of *what* and have nearly exhausted ourselves by doing so. But *how* opens the question of belief anew.

How do I believe? How do we believe? How does belief make a difference? How is the world transformed by believing? Belief will not entirely go away…Belief itself is being unfolded into a new spirit awareness as belief questions morph from *what* to *how* , from seeking information *about* God to nurturing experience *of* the divine."[162] Apparently at this point deconstruction seems to have successfully supplanted the focus from what we believe and the means used to further the message of the Gospel. The focus now is how we believe and a trend based on experience. The assertion is that experience will lend credibility to beliefs and at the same time connect with a divine dimension that will empower people to lead a more meaningful life. The "meaningful life" will in turn

---

[161] Sproul, *The Mystery of the Holy Spirit*, 166.
[162] Bass, *Christianity After Religion*, 114.

constitute an authentic living and believing in the "right way."[163]

Such ideology rejects Biblical doctrine in favor of a sensual (that is, using one's senses) experience that satisfies the desire for a tangible religion. It releases one from the perceived "doctrinal issues" that society has a problem with. The doctrinal issues represent the perceived authoritative and gender biases inherent in Scriptural doctrine.[164] No surprise here. In the book of Jude, verse 4, it states, *"For certain people have crept in unnoticed who long ago were designated for this condemnation, ungodly people, who pervert the grace of our God into sensuality and deny our Master and Lord, Jesus Christ."*

DeYoung and Kluck present it this way, "All we need is Jesus many emerging Christians cry, 'not these fancy theologies and doctrinal formulations.' Gone are sola scriptura, sin, hell, Jesus' atonement, divine judgment, the need for salvation because of man's fallen state. There's no question that Paul believed in orthodoxy. 'Follow the pattern of the sound words that you have heard from me, in the faith and love that are in Christ Jesus,' he told Timothy. *'By the Holy Spirit who dwells within us, guard the good deposit entrusted to you'* (2 Tim. 1:13-14).

Paul's message undoubtedly had a doctrinal center. There were certain propositions of fact regarding election, the incarnation, the resurrection, and the atonement that

---

[163] Ibid., 109.
[164] DeYoung and Kluck, *Why We're Not Emergent,* 108.

Paul had passed along to Timothy that also had to be preserved and protected at all costs, even if it meant suffering and death (1: 8-11)."

Conclusion

The dawning of the 21st century revealed an unprecedented attack on Christianity. The antithesis of deconstruction intended to break foundational Christian doctrine and to reconstruct it to coincide with selfish wants. The frontal attack was aided by Hegelian logic which served to change the traditional way of interpreting reality.

The new logic proves to be void of any godly semblance. Christianity has been reinterpreted from one that is shaped by foundational truths which structures our logic to beliefs based on personal sensual experiences. From objective truths to subjectiveness, the door is open for the flesh to reign. Current culture has bowed to Postmodernism and worships it as the new enlightenment for mankind. If one looks beyond what is at present, one will find a great deception. The "age of spirituality" is truly the age of spiritual adultery. Compromise or synthesis with prevailing secular demands has verily caused an adulteration of God's Word. The next chapter will discuss the ramifications of such a deception.

Chapter Twelve

ళళళ

TRUTH OR CONSEQUENCES

"We must have a Christian revolution. Love, yes. But let us understand that if we are to have it, we need to know what it is." Francis Schaeffer

The last chapter discussed an inverted logic that offers a prescription for one's "attainment of Christianity." The new logic dictates that belonging, behaving, and believing is the path to pursue in order to become a Christian. The logic represents a complete reversal of what is taught in Scripture as, believing, behaving and belonging. One has to wonder the consequences of such aberrant logic.

Scripture states;

Ps. 11:3, *"if the foundations are destroyed what can the righteous do?"*

Ps. 12, *"Save O Lord, for the godly one is gone; for the faithful have vanished from among the children of man. Everyone utters lies to his neighbor; with flattering lips and a double heart they speak. May the Lord cut off all flattering lips, the tongue that make great boasts, those who say, 'With our tongue we will prevail, our lips are with us; who is master over us?' 'Because the poor are plundered, because the needy groan, I will now arise,' says the Lord; 'I will place him in the safety for which he longs.' The words of the Lord are pure words, like silver refined in a furnace on the ground, purified seven times. You, O Lord, will keep them; you will guard us from this generation forever. On every side the wicked prowl, as vileness is exalted among the children of man.'*

Acts 19:2, *"And he said to them, 'Did you receive the Holy Spirit when you believed? And they said, 'No, we have not even heard that there is a Holy Spirit.'"*

The pressing question of the 21st century is how does one come to believe? Believing is an innate characteristic of human beings like animals that display behaviors that they are born with. Whether it is Jesus Christ, our Lord or a monkey, rat, something out of their imagination or in himself, man demonstrates a desire to believe in a deity.

When we turn to God, to know who God is and what is His character and will, the Holy Spirit is the one who reveals it to us. In 1Cor. 2:9-12, Paul writes, *"What no eye has seen, nor ear has heard, nor the heart of man*

*imagined, what God has prepared for those who love him –
these things God has revealed to us through the Holy Spirit.
For the Spirit searches everything, even the depths of God.
For who knows a person's thought except the spirit of the
person, which is in him? So also no one comprehends the
thoughts of God except the Spirit of God. Now we have
received not the spirit of the world, but the Spirit who is from
God, that we might understand the things freely given us by
God."* The work of the Holy Spirit is what transforms us, a
spiritual rebirth that enables us to <u>know who God is and to
believe in Him</u>. Through the Holy Spirit we have a
personal experience with God. Thus if the question today
is no longer what we believe but how we believe, the answer
has never changed. The answer remains the same. It is still
the Holy Spirit. He is the how!

Sadly today's theology teaches that the *how* and the
who spring from two sources: one is relationship and the
second is authenticity. As a consequence, "people trust
those whom they are friends or feel they could be friends
with…Authenticity comes through connection, personal
investment, and communal accountability, rather than
submission to systems or structures of expertise. Related
closely to friendship is the test of authenticity. Something
is true or trustworthy because it springs from good motives
and praiseworthy intentions, with results that prove to
increase happiness and make peoples' lives better.
Practicing what one preaches is a mark of spiritual truth

and humanity and humility fosters trust."[165] Practice is likened to behaving. Practice as one would in a sport in order to reach perfection in that sport. Practice though, does not bring spiritual truth, humanity, or humility that in turn fosters trust.

Through the regenerating power of the Holy Spirit our behavior changes from one that is referenced from worldly or fleshly desires to one that reflects our rebirth through Christ. The fruit of the Spirit as listed in Gal. 5: 22-26[166] serve as a model for authentic living. The authenticity comes not from ourselves but by the indwelling Holy Spirit. If we produced the "fruit" it would not be authentic, it would just be more of ourselves. But with the Holy Spirit being the producer, the fruit is genuine, thus authentic. As we take on the fruit of the Holy Spirit and reflect them on our behavior, we exemplify true authentic living.

Clearly the power of the Holy Spirit is denied. A relationship with God rests entirely on man. Hence, one's spiritual journey starts with belonging to a community, not with God's grace. Today's concept of community negates His grace, His sovereignty and authority. It rebukes God's

---

[165] Bass, *Christianity After Religion,* 115.

[166] Gal. 5: 22-26 states, "But the fruit of the Spirit is love, joy, peace, patience, kindness, goodness, faithfulness, gentleness, self-control, against such things there is not law. And those who belong to Christ Jesus have crucified the flesh with its passions and desires. If we live by the Spirit, let us walk by the Spirit. Let us not become conceited, provoking one another, envying one another."

work through the Holy Spirit "who convicts, call, draws and regenerates elect sinners."[167]

Community is important but we must stand firm to a godly definition of community of "belonging." As Paul states in Scripture, we are brothers (and sisters) in Christ. Dietrich Bonhoeffer expounds on this topic by expressing, "One is a brother to another only through Jesus Christ. I am a brother to another person through what Jesus Christ did for me and to me; the other person has become a brother to me through what Jesus Christ did for him. This fact that we are brethren only through Jesus Christ is of immeasurable significance. Not only the other person who is earnest and devout, who comes to me seeking brotherhood, must I deal within fellowship. My brother is rather that other person who has been redeemed by Christ, delivered from his sin, and called to faith and eternal life. Not what a man is in himself as a Christian, his spirituality and piety, constitutes the basis of our community. What determines our brotherhood is that man is by reason what the man is by reason of Christ. Our community with one another consists solely in what Christ has done to both of us."[168]

Furthermore, Bonhoeffer warns against those who profess something other than a community ordered by Jesus. He states, "One who wants more than Christ has established does not want Christ in brotherhood. He is

---

[167] Lawson, *The Gospel Focus of Charles Spurgeon,* 52.
[168] Bonhoeffer, *Life Together,* 25.

looking for some extraordinary social experience which he has not found elsewhere; he is bringing muddled and impure desires into Christian brotherhood.

Just at this point Christian brotherhood is threatened most often at the very start by the greatest danger of all, the danger of being poisoned at its root, the danger of confusing Christian brotherhood with some wishful idea of religious fellowship, of confounding the natural desire of the devout heart for community with the spiritual reality of Christian brotherhood. In Christian brotherhood everything depends upon its being clear right from the beginning, *first, that Christian brotherhood is not an ideal, but a divine reality. Second, that Christian brotherhood is a spiritual and not a psychic reality."*[171]

There is no error when there is a call to emulate Jesus or behave like Jesus. Since Jesus is also God, He serves us with a godly model for behavior in various situations. For the ECM proponents, Matt 5: 1-6 also known as the Sermon on the Mount is used to substantiate its model for living. They opine that if the verses of the Sermon of Mount are lived, the kingdom of God will be produced on earth. The kingdom of God is produced on earth by imitating Jesus' actions. "The rationale is that Jesus did not tell [disciples] to have faith. He pushed them into a world to practice faith. The disciples did not hope the world would change. They changed it. And in doing so, they themselves changed… When placed in the here and now, and in the context of following a spiritual path, the meaning is crystal clear: actions shape faith. Spiritual practice engender hope. Behavior opens the door for believing ... without practice, faith is but an empty promise."[169]

What are the consequences of this belief? Jesus Christ did start the kingdom of God on earth when He was incarnate. The job will be completed when He returns again on judgment day. The mistaken claim that the kingdom of God is already here predisposes one to deny hell and thus sin. Brian McLaren presents it this way, "And the Apostle John describes something equally wonderful – that at the sight of Jesus Christ, in the presence of his unmitigated brightness and unveiled glory, all the darkness [sin] in us will be banished.

How great is the love the Father has lavished on us, that we should be called children of God!"[170] According to Rob Bell, "what we find in Jesus' teaching about hell – a volatile mixture of images, pictures and metaphors that describe the very real experiences and consequences of rejecting God – given goodness and humanity."[171] "God is doing a new work through Jesus, calling all people to human solidarity. Everybody is a brother, a sister. Equals, children of God who shows no favoritism. To reject this new social order of God was to reject Jesus; the very movement of God in flesh and blood."[172] To the McLarens

---

[169] Bass, *Christianity After Religion,* 207-208.
[170] McLaren, *A New Kind of Christianity,* 129.
[171] Bell, *Love Wins,* 73.
[172] Ibid., 76.

and Bells of the world sin and the concept of hell means reflecting what mankind is not doing right now for the kingdom of God.

Therefore behaving is a practice that would bring the kingdom of God. A new social order wrought by the incarnate God. Through practices or right behavior, believing will follow and rejecting the new social order is sin. The implication, once again, is that self is first and foremost. Self retains privilege of access to God without the interruption of sin. The assertion that man can approach God without the impediment of sin goes back to the Pelagian concept that denies original sin. There is no transmission of sin after the fall from grace by Adam and Eve. The line of argument is that we are born in a state of innocence as Adam was. Sin is committed in life as a result of bad practices or behavior.

We behave because of the indwelling Holy Spirit as a result of one's faith. We belong because we share in the spiritual community of our faith in Christ.

Conclusion

The Bible is the bedrock, the foundation of Christianity and the "sword" to fight evil. God uses Scripture as the medium to speak to us. Inside the pages of the Bible God reveals to us His love, joy and wrath. Core and timeless doctrines and propositional truths are disclosed to us from which we are to live by. If these truths and the Bible as a whole are rejected as the inerrant Word of God, what are we to do as Ps 11:3 asks?

Current Christian theology teaches us that "I belong so that I can behave so that I can believe." The credo minimizes God's sovereignty, absoluteness, all knowing, eternal person. He is not to be feared as He possesses only love and, no wrath towards us. As a consequence, the downgrade of His supreme character negates our creation in His own image. It negates our purpose to glorify Him. Man comes first and man's choosing in life determines how God is worshipped. The call in Christian churches is to live the way Jesus lived. Again, there is no error in the call but delve deeper beyond the surface. What does this call truly mean? "Live the way Jesus lived" contains no real message. As Dale Van Dyke states, "Jesus lived the way He lived to fulfill the law to us… Christ is the end of the law, and if you've missed that you've missed the point. We've got to get back to the objective reality of what Christ accomplished. Moralism flat out doesn't work. It either creates Pharisees or it makes you despair."[173]

"I belong so that I can behave so that I can believe." Seriously! Really! How about "I believe so that I behave so that I belong." God explicitly states in 1 John 3:23, *"And this is his commandment, that we believe in the name of his Son Jesus Christ."* Because of our faith in God and the atoning work of Jesus Christ, we are called to be holy. 1 Peter 1:13-16 explains, *"Therefore preparing you minds for*

---

[173] DeYoung and Kluck, *Why We're Not Emergent,* 220-221.

action and being single-minded, set your hope fully on grace that will be brought to you at the revelation of Jesus Christ. As obedient children, do not be conformed to the passions of your former ignorance, but, as he who called you is holy, you are also to be holy in all your conduct, since it is written, 'You shall be holy, for I am holy.'"

The common faith that true believers have for Jesus Christ and the way they live in obedience to God is reflected in our brotherhood in Jesus and in turn in our community. 1 Cor. 1:10 we find Paul exhorting, *"I appeal to you, brothers, by the name of our Lord Jesus Christ, that all of you agree and that there be no divisions among you, but that you be united in the same mind and the same judgment."* Ps. 133 states, *"Behold, how good and pleasant it is when brothers dwell in unity! It is like the precious oil on the head, running down on the beard, on the beard of Aaron, running down on the collar of his robes! It is like the dew of Hermon, which falls on the mountains of Zion! For there the Lord has commanded the blessing, life forever."174*

Therefore do not be deceived. Beware at all times for deception comes in many forms. Even Satan comes as a "bearer of light." Make a solemn vow that "as for me, and my house, we serve the Lord."

---

174 As with all disciples of Jesus, they are considered priests or anointed ones (just like Aaron). The precious oil signifies the grace and brotherly love that is poured on each one of us. Hermon is a high hill beyond the river Jordan and the mountains of Zion which surround Jerusalem and is separated by 100 miles. The metaphor of the quiet and gentle dew represents God's love and grace which falls on His people. In turn, God's people will live in peace and love. But God being true to His word commands the greatest blessing which comes through His Son, that those in a community united by Christ shall live forever.

Praise the Lord!

I will give thanks to the Lord with my whole heart,

in the company of the upright, in the congregation.

Great are the works of the Lord,

studied by all who delight in them.

Full of splendor and majesty is his work,

and his righteousness endures forever.

He has caused his wondrous works to be remembered;

the Lord is gracious and merciful.

He provides food for those who fear him;

He remembers his covenant forever.

He has shown his people the power of his works,

in giving them the inheritance of the nations.

The works of his hands are faithful and just; all his precepts
are trustworthy; they are established forever and ever,

to be performed with faithfulness and uprightness.

He sent redemption to his people;

He has commanded his covenant forever.

Holy and awesome is his name!

The fear of the Lord is the beginning of wisdom;

all those who practice it have a good understanding.

His praise endures forever!" Ps. 111

Epilogue

"So is it with the resurrection of the dead. What is sown is perishable; what is raised is imperishable. It is sown in dishonor; it is raised in glory. It is sown in weakness; it is raised in power. It is sown in natural body; it is raised a spiritual body. If there is a natural body, there is also a spiritual body. Thus it is written, '*The first man Adam became a living being', the last Adam became a life-giving spirit. But it is not the spiritual that is first but the natural, and then spiritual. The first man was from the earth, a man of dust; the second man is from heaven. As was man of dust; so also are those who are of dust, and as is the man of heaven, so also are those who are of heaven. Just as we are borne the image of the man of dust, we shall also bear the image of the man of heaven*" (1Cor. 15:42-49).

Let's review Alfred Weber's explanation of Hegelian logic. The logic dictates that for anything to have being, its contradiction or opposite (antithesis) is necessary. A thesis is reconciled in the unity of its contradiction to produce a synthesis. The synthesis then becomes a new thesis and the process repeats itself moving towards perfection.

An example of this logic applied to Scripture is seen in 1 Cor. 15:42-49. The Bible passage tells us that what is sown by natural man is perishable. Additionally it is sown in "dishonor" and "weakness." As opposed to its contradiction, the spiritual man, sows what is "imperishable" and is "raised in glory and power." Natural man in the context of the passage is the thesis. The antithesis is the spiritual man or Jesus. Natural man is a temporal living being and its antithesis, the spiritual man is life giving. The last verse of the passage informs us that through the grace of God, there is a synthesis. "Just as we are borne the image of the man of dust, we shall also bear the image of the man of heaven," the spiritual man.

When a person repents of his/her sins and becomes a believer through the saving grace of God in the atoning work of the Jesus Christ, a transformation takes place. You can say that the person experiences a synthesis. The unity of natural man and the spiritual man which can only be reconciled through the spiritual man, enables one to embark on the path of sanctification. Sanctification is the process by which one strives to become more in the image of God. *"You therefore must be perfect, as your heavenly Father is perfect"* (Matt. 5:48).

The call from God is to reach perfection (just like secular Hegelian logic directs but without God). We can never reach perfection because we are not God, nor Jesus. Nevertheless the Lord God allows this process. "We go from strength to strength; each one appears before God in Zion" (Ps. 84:7) until the Lord call us home. The road of sanctification entail trials and tribulations as well as joys as our Lord molds us to His liking. *"We are the clay and [He is] our potter; we are all the work of [His] hand"* (Isa. 64:8). As Paul tells his fellow Corinthian believers, *"Behold! I tell you a mystery. We shall not all sleep, but we shall all be changed"* (1 Cor. 15:51).

Has Satan ever invented anything other than lies? He is incapable; he has always copied our Lord God and perverted it to suit his needs. Indeed, this book attests to the wiles of the evil one to deceive mankind and direct it to the depths of Sheol. So why not distort the logic/reasoning that God teaches us in the Bible, the logic that is designed to bring his people back to Him? In the end time, Satan has pulled out all the stops. We are therefore obligated to be aware of, understand and act to counter all and any logic/reasoning that is not of God! The last time is at hand. Know Scripture! Know God through the Holy Spirit so that the evil one may be thwarted!

www.ingramcontent.com/pod-product-compliance
Lightning Source LLC
Chambersburg PA
CBHW030928090426
42737CB00007B/354